Spanish American Music in New Mexico

THE WPA ERA

Spanish American Music in New Mexico
THE WPA ERA
Folk Songs, Dance Tunes, Singing Games, and Guitar Arrangements

Foreword by Jack Loeffler
Compiled and Edited by James Clois Smith Jr.

SUNSTONE PRESS
SANTA FE

PUBLISHER NOTES

The material in this book was taken from original sources and reflects the reproduction quality of the period. No attempts have been made to alter the appearance of these original source materials.

Readers will note that the titles of the songs in the original contents pages for each Unit often vary slightly from the actual titles inside each Unit. In the general contents pages for this book, original spellings and style have been retained in order to match the contents listings in each Unit's content page.

In *Guitar Arrangements of Spanish American Folk Songs,* page 2 of the song, "Chaparrita" was missing from the source material. In order to complete the song, the second page of this song from Unit 1 has been substituted. Any reader who has access to an original of this page is asked to contact Sunstone Press: (505) 988-4418.

The woodblock illustration that appears in various sections of this book is by Z. Kavin and originally appeared in *The Santa Fean,* Early Summer, 1941, Vol. 1, No. 10.

© 2017 by Sunstone Press
All Rights Reserved.
No part of this book may be reproduced in any form or by any electronic or mechanical means including information storage and retrieval systems without permission in writing from the publisher, except by a reviewer who may quote brief passages in a review.
Sunstone books may be purchased for educational, business, or sales promotional use.
For information please write: Special Markets Department, Sunstone Press,
P.O. Box 2321, Santa Fe, New Mexico 87504-2321.
Cover design › Vicki Ahl
Printed on acid-free paper

WWW.SUNSTONEPRESS.COM
SUNSTONE PRESS / POST OFFICE BOX 2321 / SANTA FE, NM 87504-2321 /USA
(505) 988-4418 / ORDERS ONLY (800) 243-5644 / FAX (505) 988-1025

CONTENTS

FOREWORD / Jack Loeffler / 7
THE WPA FEDERAL MUSIC PROJECT IN NEW MEXICO / Charles R. Cutter / 11
ACKNOWLEDGEMENTS / 23

Spanish American Folk Songs of New Mexico, 1936–37, Unit No. 1 / 25

Caminito / Little Road	29
La Maguana / The Itch	32
El Amor de las Mujeres / The Love of Women	34
El Borrachito / The Little Tippler	36
El Dia de tu Santo / Your Saint's Day	38
Las Campanas de Belen / The Bells of Belen	41
Me Case Con Una Pocha / I Married a 'Pocha'	43
Chaparrita / Shorty	45
Soñando / Dreaming	48
El Lirio / The Lily	51
La Ladera / The Mountain Slope	54
El Domingo la Conoci / I Met Her on Sunday	57
Corrido del Indio Victorio / Ballad of the Indian Victorio	59
Recuerdos de una Ingrata / Remembrance of an Ingrate	61
Son Tres Flores / Three Flowers	63

Spanish American Folk Songs of New Mexico, 1936–37, Unit No. 2 / 67

La Fresca Rosa / The Fresh Rose	69
La Gota / The Dewdrop	71
No Me Mires / Do Not Look At Me	74
Paso del Norte / Ballad of El Paso	77
El Ruego / The Entreaty	80
Gacela / The Doe	83
Las Tardes del Invierno / Winter Evenings	85
El Pajarillo Errante / The Errant Bird	88
La Noche Esta Serena / The Night is Serene	90
La Casita en el Cerrito / The Little House in the Mountain	93
El Punal / The Dagger	98
Valse Apasionado / The Passionate Waltz	101
En una Tarde Te Vi / One Evening I Saw You	104
El Corrido de Jose Elizoido / Ballad of Jose Elizoido	106
Los Pollos de la Capital / The Chickens from the Capitol	110
Decima del Sombrero de Petate / The Grass Hat	113
A la Puerta del Cielo / At the Gate of Heaven	116
Chimayó / Chimayo	118

Spanish American Singing Games of New Mexico, Revised 1940, Unit No. 3 / 121

Naranja Dulce / Sweet Orange _____ 125
Juan Pirulero / John Pirulero _____ 128
María Blanca / Lovely Mary _____ 130
Arre, Mi Burrito / Giddy-up, My Little Burro _____ 132
Doña Ana No Está Aquí / Lady Anne _____ 134
Rueda de San Miguel / St. Michael's Wheel _____ 137
La Tabla / The Table _____ 138
Víbora de La Mar / Sea serpent _____ 141
El Florón / The Flower _____ 143
Hilitos de Oro / Little Threads of Gold _____ 145
La Viudita de Santa Isabel / The Widow of St. Isabel _____ 150
La Huerfanita / The Little Orphan _____ 153
Ambo Gato / Ambo Gato _____ 156

Spanish American Dance Tunes of New Mexico, 1941, Unit No. 4 / 159

Amor Ardiente / Ardent Love _____ 161
Camila / Camelia _____ 163
La Chinche / The Bug _____ 164
El Chotis / The Schottisch _____ 165
Guadrilla / Quadrille
    Parte I / Part I *to Parte VII* / Part VII _____ 167–173
Cuna / Cradle _____ 174
Guadalupita / Little Guadalupe _____ 175
Indita / Indian Maid _____ 176
Jilote / "Jilote" _____ 177
Marcha Santa Ana / Santa Ana March _____ 178
El Paso Doble / The Two Step _____ 179
Polka No. 1 / Polka No. I _____ 180
Polka No. 2 / Polka No. II _____ 181
Polka No. 3 / Polka No. III _____ 182
La Raspa / The New Mexico Shuffle _____ 183
Rechumbe / "Rechumbe" _____ 184
Sombrero Blanco / White Hat _____ 185
Talean / "Talean" _____ 186
Vals de Cadena / Chain Waltz from Chimayo _____ 187
Vals de los Panos No. 1 / Vals de los Panos No. I _____ 188
Vals de los Panos No. 2 / Vals de los Panos No. II _____ 189
Vals Espanol / Spanish Waltz _____ 190
Vaquero / Cowboy _____ 192
La Varsoviana / The Varsoviana _____ 193

Guitar Arrangements of Spanish American Folk Songs, 1939 / 195

FOREWORD

by
Jack Loeffler

The high desert country of New Mexico is rippled with mountain ranges whose beveled slopes form watersheds that make life possible within this arid landscape. The human species has been part of the greater biotic community of this region for at least twelve thousand years. Throughout the millennia, human cultures have evolved either to wither, or survive and meld into an ever-changing *mestizaje* of genes and cultural characteristics shaped in large measure by the nature of this place.

In 1598 by Christian reckoning, Spanish colonists tapped tentative roots into the landscape that cradles the northern reaches of the Río Grande. They slowly adapted to the harsh environment, mingling with or combating against natives whose cultural origins extend into deep antiquity. Gradually they became one with their new homeland, and now celebrate twenty generations of presence in what is currently known as New Mexico.

As with every culture, music flows through the Hispano *ánima*, its rhythms in accord with the passage of time, its chord progressions inviting new melodic patterns, its lyrics often recalling moments in history that are otherwise forgotten. Indeed, the Hispano folk music of New Mexico is a cultural treasure trove of enormous proportion and distinguished longevity. There are still songs to be heard that were sung on the Iberian Peninsula before the "New World" was re-discovered by Europeans. There are narrative ballads that include *romances* and *corridos*, songs called *inditas* that have both European and Native American characteristics, humorous songs sometimes seemingly nonsensical called *relaciones*, poignant introspective songs and love songs known as *canciones*; there are *valses, polkas, vaqueros, chotes, varsovianas, cunas, valses de los paños, cuadrillas, valses de las escobas, trovos, décimas, cuandos, himnos, alabados* and other musical forms that have greatly enhanced the existence of the Hispano generations, that express every hue of the Hispano soul.

Until well into the twentieth century, many if not most *Nuevomexicanos* supplemented the family larder by subsistence farming, by raising cattle, sheep, goats, chickens, by hunting and fishing. Many lived as had their forbears in harmony with this harsh but beautiful homeland wherein they had found their *querencia*, their spiritual center.

However, in 1929, a great shadow fell across the land cast by the distant specter of collapsed financial institutions. *The Wall Street Journal*, a newspaper which for forty years had provided the reader with the enticing illusion of financial stability founded on the premise of growth for the sake of growth, was now used to provide some modest padding of warmth for myriad jobless, homeless, hungry and weary citizens who bedded down on park benches, or in urban alleys, and staved off hopelessness as best they could. The cities were hardest hit, and a countenance of despair marked the faces of millions of Americans.

In 1933, newly elected President Franklin Delano Roosevelt summoned ideas that might allay the financial calamity that characterized the Great Depression of the 1930s. Among the myriad programs Roosevelt initiated was the WPA, the Works Progress Administration (later re-named the Work Projects Administration) that was created to provide meaningful work to the unemployed millions throughout America. Thanks to New Mexico Governor Clyde Tingley, a masterful politician who wended his way into Roosevelt's good graces, New Mexico became the recipient of a fair proportion of federal WPA funding that supported thousands of otherwise unemployed men and women. One of the great programs to emerge was in support of the arts, and many painters, writers and musicians were employed to pursue their respective art forms.

Helen Chandler Ryan was appointed director of the Federal Music Project (FMP) in New Mexico that lasted from 1936–1943. In 1939, it was re-named as the New Mexico Music Project, and by 1942, the name was changed yet again to War Services Program—Music Phase. The focus of this project was "music education, performance, and preserving of local musical heritage, especially Hispanic folk music." Under Ryan's direction and that of her co-administrators, musicians and folklorists collected songs and other material that otherwise might have been lost.

The transcribed folk songs were mimeographed and distributed to teachers who taught both singers and instrumentalists who then presented the music in public performances. This music project not only funded fieldworkers, it also brought music to the people of the villages of New Mexico in a time when little else was available to lift the hearts of *la gente*.

In the volume that follows, ninety-one folksongs collected between 1936 and 1941 are assembled in five separate units. The first three units in this volume are comprised of a series of Hispano folk songs with transcribed melodies and English translations of lyrics. Of great interest is the introduction written by the late Arthur L. Campa, himself one of New Mexico's pioneer lore-trovers. He is part of a venerable lengthening lineage of folklorists, ethnomusicologists and aural historians that includes Aurelio Espinosa, Juan B. Rael, Mela Sedillo, Dolores Gonzales, Vicente Mendoza, Rubén Cobos, John D. Robb, Jenny Wells Vincent, Richard Stark, Reed Cooper, Anita Gonzalez Thomas, Cipriano Vigil, Roberto Mondragon, Frank McCulloch, Marta Weigle, Peter White, Enrique Lamadrid, Brenda Romero, Ken Keppler, Jeanie McClerie, Claude Stephenson, Tomás Lozano, Peter Garcia, and others.

One of the milestones in Unit 1 (1936–37), Unit 2 (1936–37) and Unit 3 (1940) of this volume is that both lyrics and notated melodies are included. The melodies presented herein were transcribed and arranged by Aurelio Armendariz who, we are told, collected many of the songs himself. This is significant in that few melodies of Hispano folksongs were transcribed and presented in earlier publications. Fortunately, musical notation of Hispano folk music is available in many subsequent publications. Over the last several decades, recordings of this music have been produced on 78 and 45 RPM records, LP albums, cassettes, CDs, and MP3 and other digital downloads.

Unit 4 (1940) of this volume is a collection of thirty Hispano dance songs, some of which remain popular even now. Indeed, since 1975 I have recorded versions of all but four of the dance songs that appear here. For the most part, the melodies were performed on violins and guitars. However mandolins and button accordions gradually gained prominence during the twentieth century. The *baile*, or dance remains an important social event throughout rural New Mexico.

Many of the dance forms and accompanying melodies contained in this section arrived in New Mexico via Mexico City from the salons of Paris in the 1860s when Maximilian was emperor of Mexico. As the story goes, Maximilian's wife, Carlotta was a friend of Eugenie, wife of French Emperor Napoleon III. When Eugenie became enthralled with a dance and melody in Paris, the music would waft across the Atlantic, pass overland to Mexico City to be celebrated by Carlotta and the regional high society, and thereafter wend northward along *El Camino Real de Tierra Adentro* to Santa Fe. One of the most popular folk dances, *La Varsoviana* is a perfect example of this. It apparently originated as a folk dance in the Plains of Mazoszwe near Warsaw, Poland, hence its name that translates as "the Lady from Warsaw." It was ostensibly popularized by a dance master, Desiree, in the Parisian salons, and can still be heard a century and a half later performed by *viejitos* in the Hispano villages of northern New Mexico. It is known to many of us as "Put Your Little Foot."

Unit 5 (1939), although not "numbered" as such, is entitled "Guitar Arrangements of Spanish American Folk Songs." These arrangements were penned by Eudora Garrett and are based largely on the methods taught by Tarrega who was highly regarded as a Spanish guitarist. This method was adopted by the Federal Music Project to be used throughout New Mexico.

The first part of Unit 5 is comprised of a concise but inclusive text describing the fundamentals of performing on the Spanish guitar. It was intended that any student who assiduously pursued guitar performance utilizing this method would gain proficiency and even mastery of the instrument. The second half includes eleven songs arranged for guitar that were popular during the Great Depression.

Many of the songs presented throughout this volume appear in the archives of later collectors, however many other songs would have been relegated to obscurity had they not been collected in the 1930s.

The Great Depression ended after 1941 when the United States entered the Second World War. A disproportionately high ratio of *Nuevo Mexicanos* were drafted, or otherwise enlisted in the Armed Forces. Many of them perished in the Bataan Death March in the Philippines, thus tearing an enormous rent in the fabric of New Mexican Hispano culture.

We are fortunate to have this taste of Hispano music of New Mexico from the early twentieth century. This publication, offered by Sunstone Press nearly three-quarters of a century after the initial presentation, is more than welcome. It is integral and vital to the repertoire of musical lore that greatly embellishes New Mexico's heritage. This collection is part of the phenomenal repertoire of music that emanates from the heart of one of the great and distinguished cultures of our homeland.

THE WPA FEDERAL MUSIC PROJECT IN NEW MEXICO

by
Charles R. Cutter
from
New Mexico Historical Review, Volume 61, Number 3, July 1986

As victims of the Great Depression of the 1930s, American artists were not exceptional. But as a group writers, actors, artists, and musicians were among the first to experience hard times since "luxuries" such as art and entertainment were the first things cut back in times of economic hardship. Many musicians were forced to give up their professional endeavors and seek whatever available employment they could find. It was in this prevailing atmosphere of despair that musicians throughout the country found a new patron in the federal government. Under the auspices of the Works Progress Administration, the Federal Music Project provided a variety of jobs for unemployed musicians.

In New Mexico, as elsewhere in the country, the impact of the Federal Music Project (FMP) was largely beneficial. Local circumstances, however, created different needs that were met both imaginatively and energetically by the state's FMP director, Helen Chandler Ryan, and project employees. Although generally ignored, the era of the Federal Music Project forms an interesting and important chapter in the history of New Mexico's musical community.

Helen Chandler Ryan in 1946. Courtesy of the Ryan family.

Among the many agencies created by President Franklin D. Roosevelt to cope with the economic devastation of the Great Depression was the Works Progress Administration. On May 6, 1935, Executive Order 7034 established the WPA as an independent agency, pursuant to the Emergency Relief Appropriation Act of 1935.[1] The philosophy of the WPA, headed by Harry Hopkins, was to avoid the "dole," preferring instead to provide work-relief for America's unemployed by creating worthwhile jobs at various levels, from unskilled to white collar.

Perhaps it was Roosevelt's patrician sense of noblesse oblige that inclined him favorably to the role of government as friend of the arts. Certainly his background had provided him with some knowledge of, and appreciation for, fine arts. Possibly it was his wish to share this appreciation with the common people, or he may have felt obligated to help artists as a group. Judging from the stated aims of the Federal Arts Projects—to provide work and serve the community—both factors played a part in the decision to offer help. Whatever the reasons, in July 1935, the WPA organized the Division of Professional and Service Projects under the direction of Jacob Baker. Within this division was created Federal Project Number One, commonly known simply as Federal One, which consisted of four main subdivisions devoted to music, drama, literature, and art. Funding began in October of the same year, and the WPA initiated the federal government's venture into the world of artistic patronage shortly thereafter.[2]

Despite the success of some programs, especially that of music, opposition to FDR's New Deal, and Federal One in particular, mounted. Many felt that the Theatre Project was far too radical, and it became the target of conservative attacks in Congress. Consequently, Federal One was terminated in September 1939. In a reorganization of the program, the Theatre Project ceased and all other projects fell under the general designation of the WPA Art Program. Changes in operating procedure, designed to weaken the program, greatly altered the nature of activities of the music program. Local or state sponsorship of at least 25 percent was now required. More damaging was the "eighteen month" clause providing that no individual be allowed on project relief rolls for any longer than one and a half years. This especially hurt the continuity and quality of projects of a highly professional nature, such as symphony orchestras.[3]

Throughout the country the Federal Music Project functioned in much the same way, though regional and local variation did exist. Named to head the project was Dr. Nikolai Sokoloff, former conductor of the Cleveland Symphony Orchestra and respected music educator. Sokoloff's emphasis on professionalism resulted in the formation of several highly acclaimed symphony orchestras comprised of WPA employees. It also brought criticism from many for his neglect of, and disdain for, community oriented music programs which featured folk or popular musicians.[4] Partly because of this conflict, Sokoloff resigned in 1939. His successor, Earl V. Moore, gave much more attention to promoting music as an amateur activity.[5]

Despite administrative problems, the FMP achieved remarkable success and, more importantly, public acceptance. Within nine months of its inception the project boasted an enrollment of more than 15,000 musicians nationwide who otherwise would have been unemployed, "their horns untootled."[6] After one full year of operation the musicians employed by the music project increased to over 17,000 with work in 159 symphony and concert orchestras, 89 bands, 25 chamber music ensembles, 133 dance, theatre and novelty groups, 35 vocal groups, and 258 teaching projects. There also existed programs for copyists, arrangers, binders, tuners, and instrument repairmen, as well as work for nearly 350 persons in administrative capacities of the project.[7] The national Federal Music Project was a wide-ranging ambitious endeavor.

Many musicians were already on work-relief when the project began, most of them working as laborers.[8] "Able musicians were swinging picks and shovels on labor projects, their hands toughening and all but losing their essential sensitivity."[9] One of the first steps taken by the project was to set up audition boards to evaluate the musical capacity of applicants. Naturally, standards of musicianship varied from place to place, but there was a firm insistence upon technical proficiency. In fact, Sokoloff's standards were at first so high that many professional musicians found themselves unqualified for the program. Pressures from groups such as the American Federation of Music forced Sokoloff to recognize the fact that not all professional musicians were of symphony caliber.[10] By giving jobs as musicians to those who qualified the project eased the tight labor market in two ways. Not only did musicians find work, but others took their places as laborers in less esoteric work-relief projects.

The big music centers of the country tended to emphasize large symphony orchestras and often had distinguished conductors, such as Leopold Stokowski, who volunteered their services to the program. Smaller population centers supported lesser known figures and often emphasized regional folklore or musical instruction.[11] At every level, however, talented men and women found a much needed avenue to pursue their musical careers. Like a number of important American painters, the federal government patronized these musicians during the lean years of the Great Depression.[12]

Perhaps the most important and unexpected result of the Federal Music Project was the great stimulus it gave to the appreciation of music by the general American public. In the first nine months of the project alone, some twenty million persons attended the government-sponsored concerts. Just as important, hundreds of thousands of Americans, adults and children, eagerly enrolled in various instructional programs offered by FMP teachers.[13] Americans seemed to favor the work being done by the WPA Federal Music Project, not only for the employment opportunities for musicians, but also for its entertainment and artistic value. Wrote one music critic:

> The Federal Music Project of the WPA has done noble work for music in America. In fact, its labors in the cause of creative music are unique. Never before has there been so wholesale an exposure of a nation's creative sources.[14]

Among the states of the Rocky Mountain West, New Mexico was fortunate in having one of the most imaginative and dynamic FMP directors. Appointed on January 1, 1936, Helen Chandler Ryan served as head of the New Mexico project until just before the program ended in 1943.[15] Operating from her headquarters at 1403 West Central Avenue in Albuquerque, her tireless efforts on behalf of the FMP won praise from colleagues both in and out of state.

A special set of problems confronted Ryan in the initial stages of the program. Since allocation of federal funds was based on the number of musicians and music projects within a state, New Mexico's small population meant less money. With Albuquerque as the largest city (about 35,000 inhabitants) New Mexico was hard pressed to compete with states that had cities like Los Angeles, Chicago, or New York (which alone had two full WPA symphony orchestras and employed nearly 700 musicians.)[16] Ryan wisely decided not to imitate programs of the larger states, but set out to develop a project better suited to New Mexico's circumstances.

Whereas other mountain states, particularly Utah and Colorado, spent considerable effort in supporting fine performing symphony orchestras, no professional WPA performing unit existed in New Mexico. Instead, the state FMP limited its sponsorship to musical groups that performed under the leadership of so-called "instructor-directors" employed by the WPA.[17] Unlike regular WPA performing units, these groups were permitted to charge admission for their concerts since members were not on the federal payroll. The only stipulation was that the instructor-director donate the time spent at performances.[18]

A surprising variation in musical styles characterized New Mexico's FMP presentations. The most uniquely Southwestern of the performing groups organized and instructed by WPA teachers were the tipica orchestras that likewise existed in Arizona and Texas.[19] Playing the Hispanic music of the region, several such groups performed in New Mexico, including the Children's Tipica Orchestra of Albuquerque, led by Pedro Valles, and a similar group under the direction of Pablo Mares in Las Vegas. This second group performed frequently at fiestas and other public functions in the Santa Fe area. Another well-known group which played Hispanic folk music was the guitar ensemble of the Hernández brothers of Bernalillo.[20] The New Mexico FMP proudly capped 1938 by presenting *Los Pastores*, a traditional Hispanic nativity play, performed by children under the guidance of music project teachers at Santa Fe's historic Palace of the Governors.[21]

As with the Hispanic music, most performances sponsored by the New Mexico FMP were of a popular nature. City parks, public schools, hospitals, and churches served as sites for presentations. Various community concert bands, choral groups, "Anglo-folk" ensembles, and a few jazz groups performed regularly throughout the state. Albuquerque's Junior Community Band reportedly played two concerts a week during the month of June 1938. The Española Community Band was equally active, giving performances in Taos, Chama, Puye, and Parkview.[22] Both Albuquerque and Roswell had Negro spiritual vocal groups, and Don Lesmen, a long-time Albuquerque musician, recalls that the San Isidro CCC jazz band he led often played at the "concert in the park" series in Albuquerque. An accordion band developed by the New Mexico FMP so excited Senator Carl Hatch that he sought to book the group at the nation's capital. Some 736 free public concerts under WPA sponsorship were given in New Mexico in the first two years of the project's existence.[23]

Of the other mountain states, only Arizona came close to approximating New Mexico's commitment to the idea of "music for the people." Although Utah and Colorado symphony orchestras gave numerous public performances gratis or at greatly reduced prices, their real emphasis was clearly on "artistic" rather than popular music. When one Colorado group attempted to lighten its program, it received a sharp reprimand from the national office warning against including such numbers as "Mr. Krevas and His Musical Bottles" or Miss Matlick's "Whistling Novelty."[24] New Mexico sidestepped this difficulty by not having any professional performing unit and by designating all groups as "community activity groups." In this way, they were free to perform the music they desired.[25]

Though performances were a major part of the FMP, in New Mexico other aspects of the project had greater impact. Perhaps reflective of Ryan's training in the field of music education, one of the most important contributions of the New Mexico project was in music instruction. Co-sponsored by school districts, many of them rural, the WPA offered instruction through the schools in twenty-three of the state's thirty-one counties. By August 1939, music education reached sixty-two schools where music had never been provided by local boards of education. Belen, for example, started its first school band in 1936 under the direction of music project employee Bennett Shacklett.[26] As a gesture to private instructors who feared losing students to the WPA, children were required to submit a form showing their parents' inability to pay for lessons.[27]

Other institutions also served as centers for FMP education. As an extracurricular activity, a number of Civilian Conservation Corps camps offered music instruction. Because the military administered the CCC, some of the music programs were run by army personnel. Other CCC camps, however, went through the state FMP to hire their band leaders.[28] The National Youth Administration Girls' and Boys' Camps and Girls' Welfare Home in Albuquerque, likewise, offered WPA music classes.[29]

Instruction was not only for school children. As part of the folklore project, teacher-directors trekked from community to community organizing vocal groups and giving instruction in the use of traditional instruments of New Mexico such as the guitar and violin. In Roswell and Las Cruces, several black churches combined to co-sponsor two instructor-directors from California who headed several Negro spiritual groups. Response from participants and community to these two musicians, Carrie Daniels and Arthur Walker, was enthusiastic and the work accomplished "very gratifying."[30] Even the inmates at the New Mexico State Penitentiary benefited from the WPA Music Project. A penitentiary orchestra under FMP direction afforded a figurative escape for the men who played as well as entertainment for the rest of the inmates.[31]

An excellent example of Ryan's enthusiasm and commitment to the educational aspect of the FMP was the Work Conference of Federal Music Teachers which she organized in March 1939. Held at the University of New Mexico, the three-day session featured workshops, demonstrations, and lectures designed to instruct and inspire the project teachers of New Mexico. So great was respect for her among colleagues that prominent music educators outside the project took part in the conference and one Albuquerque music store owner, Bernie May, offered to accommodate visiting teachers in his own home.[32]

New Mexico thus differed from other states in the region by emphasizing music education, especially in rural areas. While Colorado, Utah, and Arizona offered performances for school children, these projects did not actively promote actual musical instruction to the extent demonstrated in New Mexico. Ryan's instructional approach won praise from National Director Earl V. Moore, who felt that New Mexico's program "should be extended to . . . nearby states which have similar rural problems."[33]

Across the country, the Great Depression years were marked by an inward-looking nationalism that stressed the unique features of American cultural life. New Mexico's FMP reflected this general trend.[34] Indeed, one of the most ambitious projects on the state level, and certainly the most conspicuous in a national context, was the collection of traditional Hispanic folklore. Director Ryan, like so many before and since, was fascinated by the simple yet beautiful melodies of the Hispanic community. Under her impetus the project avidly sought to preserve these tunes.

WPA employees from both the music and writers' projects set out to collect as many folk songs from as many sources as possible, usually from older Hispanics. Long isolated because of rugged terrain, poor roads, an absence of electronic media, and perhaps a certain mistrust of the Anglo world, many villages of northern New Mexico still maintained some archaic vestiges of Spanish culture.

Not only speech patterns, but many of the songs sung by these hardy people had died out in both Spain and Mexico yet were still part of the New Mexican tradition.[35]

Having composed the tunes, FMP workers scored the musical notation along with accompanying words, cut stencils, and supplied mimeographed copies to music project teachers in the state.[36] One tipica orchestra from El Paso eventually recorded two of these numbers for the National Youth Administration using the arrangements of the New Mexico project.[37]

This dimension of the project, carried out in cooperation with the state's Federal Writers Project, received considerable attention both in and out of state. New Mexico's effort to collect and revive Hispanic folk music prompted national folk festivals director Sarah Gertrude Knott to remark in 1939 that "there is in New Mexico a finer integration of music project activities with the life of the people than in any other part of the United States than I have visited."[38]

Presentations of folklore such as *Los Pastores* and the tipica concerts have been mentioned. A frequent co-sponsor of these events was the League of United Latin American Citizens (LULAC) who understandably supported the spread of Hispanic culture through the FMP. A typical program presented under LULAC patronage in 1936 featured "songs and dances handed down from generation to generation in New Mexico from Spanish ancestors."[39]

Besides public performances and group instruction of folk music, the New Mexico FMP also published some of the songs collected by project employees. Significantly, all five of the agency's publications dealt in one way or another with the Hispanic music of the region. Federal Music Project Unit Number 1 (1936-1937) was entitled "Spanish-American Folk Songs of New Mexico." FMP Unit Number 2 carried the same title and dates but offered a different selection of tunes. A third publication, printed in 1939, was a "Guitar Method with Guitar Arrangements of Spanish-American Folk Songs of New Mexico." Federal Music Project Unit Number 3 appeared in 1940 as "Spanish-American Singing Games of New Mexico," and reappeared two years later as a formal publication under the title *The Spanish-American Song and Game Book*, a joint venture with the state's Writers Project. A final publication, "Spanish-American Dance Tunes of New Mexico," comprised Unit Number 4 and was published in 1941. [The incorrect date of 1942 was given in the original article.]

**Illustration from *The Spanish-American Song and Game Book*
(New York: A. S. Barnes and Company, 1942.)**

With the advent of World War II, the Federal Music Project declined in importance throughout the country. By 1940 FMP groups had begun to play for the entertainment of troops in several areas. Once the nation actually entered into hostilities, all efforts of the WPA went to the war cause.[40] New Mexico differed little from other music projects in this respect. The plan adopted by the state FMP as of June 1942 stated that the project would only "operate in places where there are Military establishments and only for [the] War Effort." In May 1942 the music project sponsored a city-wide contest at Barelas Community Center in

Albuquerque to discover musical talent for locally stationed troops. Other activities included performances at the Veterans Hospital, entertainment of troop trains, and a "half-hour program at the State-Wide Price Control meeting" where the state director led the singing of the Star Spangled Banner.[41] The Federal Music Program came to a quiet end on June 30, 1943 when Congress terminated the Federal Works Administration.

Like the national Federal Music Project, the agency's impact on New Mexico was largely beneficial. New Mexico, however, differed from other areas, even other states in the region, in several important ways. Realizing that New Mexico's small allocation of federal funds could not support a salaried professional symphony as in Utah and Colorado, Ryan sought to spread the direct financial benefits around the state to different types of musicians, both performers and instructors. Though funding and employee numbers were comparatively small (never exceeding thirty musicians), the project nevertheless offered much needed employment. As one Albuquerque saxophone player succinctly phrased it, "The WPA was a good thing, man; times were bad and it gave us musicians a chance to work."[42] Besides providing actual jobs, the project served to boost the morale of musicians and kept up their professional skills. Undoubtedly, it helped raise the flagging spirits of New Mexicans in general since they were treated to free quality entertainment.

Former FMP employees have recounted numerous stories of underprivileged children getting their first taste of music participation, underscoring another benefit of the program. At Civilian Conservation Corps camps, rural schools, or community activities, youngsters had a chance to experience the thrill of playing an instrument, something they would ordinarily have been denied. A number of schools, including Belen, trace their music education program to the WPA.[43]

Some effects of the project became apparent later; many musicians gained valuable experience as WPA workers that helped them in their subsequent careers. K. L. Higgins, a long-time respected music educator with the Albuquerque Public Schools, acquired teaching experience in the summer music camps funded by the FMP. Bennett Shaklett moved directly from his project assignment in Belen to head that school district's first music education program. Similarly, Don Lesmen's stint as director of a CCC jazz group aided in his later career as leader of various Albuquerque jazz ensembles.

New Mexico's Federal Music Project is characterized by a conspicuous lack of ethnic or racial prejudice in its programs. The emphasis on Hispanic music has been noted, but even groups not specializing in this area were often directed by, and included, a large number of persons of Spanish ancestry. Blacks were likewise represented in groups such as Albuquerque's Junior Community Band, as well as Negro spiritual groups. The music project thus served to promote ethnic diversity in the state.

The music project also had an impact on the study of New Mexican folklore. While there had been scattered interest from many different quarters in collecting Hispanic folklore and folk songs, it was under the direction of the federal government that the first systematic and coordinated efforts were made to record and revive New Mexico's rich folk tradition.[44] The WPA brought together both the collectors and the participants and served as a catalyst for a concerted effort to collect, preserve, and teach various aspects of Hispanic folk art in New Mexico. The high caliber of this effort is demonstrated in the presence of Arthur L. Campa and Rubén Cobos, major Hispanic folklorists at the University of New Mexico, as participants in the WPA program, though not as employees of the music project. Later research on the subject followed the trend set in the WPA era: folklorists looked to the government to fund their efforts.[45]

It is apparent that New Mexico's Federal Music Project offered a wide variety of employment opportunities and community programs which helped relieve the economic distress of the state's musicians and heightened musical appreciation among the general public. Helen Chandler Ryan's ability to transmit project ideals into workable programs that maximized New Mexico's strong points benefited musicians and non-musicians alike. When viewed in terms of its immediate and long-range achievements, the Federal Music Project in New Mexico appears to have been an overwhelming success.

NOTES

1. Executive Order 7034, May 6, 1935.
2. Francis O'Connor, *Federal Art Patronage, 1933–1943* (College Park, Maryland: University of Maryland, 1966), 27.
3. William F. McDonald, *Federal Relief Administration and the Arts* (Columbus: Ohio State University Press, 1969), 616; O'Connor, *Patronage*, 28.
4. Neal Cannon, "Art For Whose Sake: The Federal Music Project of the WPA," Ray Browne, Larry N. Landrum and William K. Bottorf, eds., *Challenges in American Culture* (Bowling Green, Ohio: Bowling Green University Popular Press, 1970), 85-98.
5. McDonald, *Federal Relief*, 605-10.
6. "WPA Melody for Twenty Millions," *Literary Digest*, 122 (September 19, 1936), 22.
7. "The Federal Music Project," *New Republic*, 89 (November 11, 1936), 48; National Archives and Records Center, Record Group 69, "Record of Program Operation and Accomplishment: The Federal Music Project, 1935 to 1943," 46, WPA Federal Music Project (hereafter cited as FMP), Record Group 69, National Archives.
8. McDonald, *Federal Relief*, 584-600, gives details concerning pre-WPA work relief for musicians.
9. "WPA Melody," 22.
10. McDonald, *Federal Relief*, 610.
11. "WPA Melody," 22.
12. William Schuman and Roger L. Stevens, *Economic Pressures and the Future of the Arts* (New York: Free Press, 1979), 80.
13. "Federal Music Project," *Current History*, 48-49 (September 1938), 43; FMP, "Record of Program Operation and Accomplishment," 360, FMP.
14. Samuel Shotzinoff, as quoted in "WPA Melody," 22.
15. Memo from Ellen S. Woodward to Jay duVon, n.d., 651.311 New Mexico, FMP.
16. "Pride of New York City WPA," *Newsweek*, 17 (March 31, 1941), 63.
17. Helen Ryan to Nikolai Sokoloff, February 1, 1938, 651.311 New Mexico, FMP.
18. Ryan to Sokoloff, April 6, 1938, *ibid*.
19. Narrative Reports, Arizona 1939, FMP.
20. Narrative Reports, New Mexico 1939, FMP; personal interview with K. L. Higgins, Albuquerque, October 1983; personal interview with Concha Ortiz y Pino de Kleven, Albuquerque, April 1982; personal interview with Higgins, Albuquerque, April 1982.
21. Ryan to Sokoloff, December 10, 1938; 651.311 New Mexico, FMP.
22. Interview with Higgins, October 6, 1983; personal interviews with Don Lesmen, Albuquerque, March 1982 and November 1983; Narrative Reports, New Mexico 1938, FMP.
23. Interview with Lesmen, March 1982; Narrative Reports, New Mexico 1942, FMP; memo from duVon to Douglas Brooks, July 11, 1941, 651.311 New Mexico, FMP; WPA Writers Program, *New Mexico: A Guide to the Colorful State* (Albuquerque: University of New Mexico Press, 1945), 147.
24. Alma Munsell to Ivan Miller, February 26, 1936, 651.311 Colorado, FMP.
25. Sokoloff to Ryan, June 17, 1938, 651.311 New Mexico, FMP.
26. Narrative Reports, New Mexico 1939, FMP; personal interview with Bennett Shacklett, Roswell, December 1, 1983.

27. Ryan to Sokoloff, October 11, 1938, 651.311 New Mexico, FMP.
28. Personal interviews with Charles G. Ryan, Albuquerque, April 1982 and November 1983; interview with Lesmen, November 1983; Narrative Reports, New Mexico 1939, FMP.
29. Narrative Reports, New Mexico 1938, FMP.
30. "Spanish-American Folk Songs of New Mexico," Works Progress Administration, Federal Music Project, Unit Number 1, 1936–37; interview with Charles G. Ryan, April 1982; Healy to Woodward, June 25, 1938, 651.311 New Mexico, FMP.
31. Narrative Reports, New Mexico 1939, FMP.
32. Narrative Reports, New Mexico 1939, FMP; personal interview with Bernie May, Albuquerque, December 1, 1983.
33. Ryan to Earl V. Moore, September 12, 1939, 651.311 New Mexico, FMP.
34. Richard D. McKinzie, *The New Deal for Artists* (Princeton: Princeton University Press, 1973), x.
35. Personal interview with John Donald Robb, Albuquerque, March 1982.
36. "Spanish-American Folk Songs," Unit Number 1; personal interviews with Virginia LaPine, Albuquerque, April 1982 and November 1983.
37. Ryan to Margaret Valiant, May 5, 1941, 651.311 New Mexico, FMP.
38. As quoted in Lorin Brown, *Hispano Folklife of New Mexico* (Albuquerque: University of New Mexico Press, 1978), 242.
39. *Albuquerque Journal*, June 4, 1936, p. 7.
40. McDonald, *Federal Relief*, 616.
41. *Albuquerque Journal*, May 7, 1942, p. 7; Report of May 26, 1942, 651.311 New Mexico, FMP.
42. Interview with Lesmen, March 1982.
43. Nearly all of the interviewees had stories of this nature. Bennett Shacklett began the music program in the Belen schools.
44. Personal interview with Grace Edminster, Albuquerque, March 1982; interview with Charles G. Ryan, April 1982.
45. Interview with Robb, March 1982.

ACKNOWLEDGEMENTS

Sunstone Press expresses gratitude to Michael Kelly, Director of University of New Mexico Libraries' Center for Southwest Research/Special Collections, for giving us access to materials in their collection; Laura Holt for her excellent research; Kathryn A. Flynn, Executive Director, National New Deal Preservation Association, for her enthusiasm and support; and special gratitude to the National New Deal Preservation Association for helping make this project possible.

Spanish American Folk Songs of New Mexico, 1936–37, Unit No. 1

INTRODUCTION

By

Professor A. L. Campa
Director of Research in Folklore
and
Professor in Modern Languages
University of New Mexico

※※※

No other form of folk production is so revealing of temperament and subjectivism as the folk song. Since for its presentation a collective endeavor of society is not necessary, in it may be found an individual interpretation and uninhibited expression that other forms of folklore do not possess. The popular song in New Mexico had its beginning in the ballads of the sixteenth century, but various adaptations have taken place in the last three centuries—adaptations that have changed considerably the structure of the song though they have maintained the spirit of trovadoresque compositions.

A large number of songs have come from Mexico in the course of the last century, but this northern region has exercised its influence upon them giving them the stamp of New Mexican folk song. Woven in the texture of popular singing may be found that archaic, the traditional, in addition to those compositions that have sprung from the soil of this western state. We have now an endless repertoire dealing with every manifestation of life, expressing every fine nuance of emotion of our American population that now makes its contribution towards a culture that because of its diversity is unequaled anywhere else. The work of the Federal Government in helping to collect, record, and perpetuate the melodies of our Spanish Southwest is making a contribution for which we shall be thankful in years to come. The symphonic epic of America will be composed of songs that include every region and particularly those regions whose traditions date beyond the settlements on the eastern shores.

We are not dealing with a revival of obsolete material but, rather, with a preservation of something that is alive today. Not only that, but a selective preservation of material that because of its genuineness and its beauty we cannot afford to neglect.

THE FUNCTIONING OF FOLKLORE PROJECTS
Under
Works Progress Administration
Federal Music Project in New Mexico

By

Helen Chandler Ryan
State Director

**

The fact that New Mexico has such a rich heritage of Hispanic-American folklore, which for lack of recording is being lost to present and future generations, has prompted the setting up of folklore collecting and singing projects under W.P.A. Federal Music to help preserve almost forgotten tunes and verses for posterity.

These so-called folklore projects are functioning in several different ways. First, the Hispanic-Americans, who are employed, collect as many folk songs as possible from the old native residents. In several instances these singers have been centenarians or older. Many of the songs deal with historic events; others are "romances" with sometimes a pathetic, sometimes a humorous vein. These are written down in music notation with the accompanying words and are then arranged in simple Mexican folk manner for voice and piano or guitar. After this, stencils are cut and mimeographed copies are made for distribution among the various singing groups. No attempt at change or elaboration of these melodies is permitted since it is an unalterable rule that the songs must remain in the original form in which they are sung. Often interesting differences are found in the same song as it is sung in different sections of the state, thus proving the rule that songs change by use and are influenced by environment.

In order to keep alive these folk songs among our people, singing groups have been organized under competent teacher-directors and these old songs are taught together with many more familiar ones. Programs are given by these groups frequently and are greatly enjoyed not only by the Hispanic-Americans but by a rapidly increasing American public as well, to whom these songs are a new experience. Many of the folk songs are intended to be used in dancing and these lend an interesting variety to the programs. Effort is being made now to have large community singing groups meet fortnightly where these songs will be sung and thus reach a larger number of people who actually will learn to sing them.

Another phase of the folklore projects is the teaching of string instruments to those otherwise unable to receive this instruction. Thus Tipica Orchestra groups are organized to play the folk songs and many children are taught the guitar which is the most popular accompanying instrument for folk singing. Some of the folk songs which are being taught were recorded and transcribed by the folklore department of the University of New Mexico under the Rockerfeller foundation. The University has been most co-operative and helpful in allowing us to use their material. We are particularly indebted to Professor A. L. Campa, head of the folklore department, who has generously given his time and many helpful suggestions.

New Mexico is planning an elaborate Cuarto Centennial in 1940, commemorating the entrance of Coronado into New Mexico. It is expected that the attention of the nation and the world will be focused here at that time. Since the celebration is to be worked out in the form of authentic, historical pageants, much can be done by this folklore project to help - both in the way of research for the authentic music which was sung at that time and in teaching these songs to the hundreds and thousands of people who will participate.

The fifteen songs submitted under this cover comprise the first unit of Hispanic-American folk songs which are being recorded. Other units will follow later.

TABLE OF CONTENTS

Caminito	- "Little Road"
La Maguana	- "The Itch"
El Amor de las Mujeres	- "The Love of Women"
El Borrachito	- "The Little Tippler"
El Dia de tu Santo	- "Your Saint's Day"
Las Campanas de Belen	- "The Bells of Belen"
Me Case Con Una Pocha	- "I married a 'Pocha'"
Chaparrita	- "Shorty"
Soñando	- "Dreaming"
El Lirio	- "The Lily"
La Ladera	- "The Mountain Slope"
El Domingo la Conoci	- "I Met Her on Sunday"
Corrido del Indio Victorio	- "Ballad of the Indian Victorio"
Recuerdos de una Ingrata	- "Remembrance of an Ingrate"
Son Tres Flores	- "Three Flowers"

CAMINITO

Caminito tan bonito y derechito
Chiquitito para andar
Si me ves a Consuelito
Si me ves a mi amorcito
No me dejes de avisar.

Caminito tan bonito
Que alcabo ay vas a parar
Si es que ves a mi amorcito
Si es que ves a Consuelito
No me dejes de avisar.

Te voy a enseñar mis milpas
Mis ovejas y mi buey
Y dile que si la espero
Y dile que si me quedo
Yo me muero en el "highway"

CAMINITO
(Little Road)

Little road, so pretty and straight
So little to walk on
If you see my Consuelito
If you see my little love
Don't fail to let me know (about it)

Little Road, so pretty
Anyway, that's where you end
Should you happen to see my little love
Should you happen to see my Consuelito
Don't fail to let me know (about it)

I am going to show you my cornfields
My sheep and my ox
And tell her that if I wait for her
And tell her that if I am rejected
I will die on the highway

****

Caminito is a love song. It was sung by Mr. Salomon Garcia from Arroyo Hondo, New Mexico, a little Village near Taos, New Mexico. This song is also a message of love, very similar to "La Ladera" in its meaning.

LA MAGUANA

Entre la Petra y la Juana
Pusieron un tendejon
La Petra vendia maguana
Y Juana la comezon
Tra la ra la la la
Tra la ra la la

Ursula que andas haciendo
Con tus zapatos de lana
Visitando mis enfermos
Que estan malos de maguana
Tra la etc.

Si vas al arroyo chico
No vayas de mala gana
Porque anda una enfermedad
Que le dicen la maguana
Tra la etc.

Si vas al arroyo chico
No vayas de mala gana
Porque anda una enfermedad
Que le dicen la maguana
Tra la etc.

Las muchachas de Chihuahua
Se levantan de manana
Y una a la otra se pregunta
Come te va de maguana
Tra la etc.

LA MAGUANA
(The Itch)

Between Petra and Juan
They set up a store
Petra sold the itch
And Juana the desire to scritch
Tra la ra la la la
Tra la ra la la la

Ursula what are you doing
With your woolen shoes
Visiting the sick
Who are sick with the itch
Tra la ra la la la
Tra la ra la la la

If you go the little "arroyo"
Do not go because you have to
Because a sickness is going around
That they call the itch
Tra la ra la la la
Tra la ra la la la

The girls from Chihuahua
Get up early in the morning
And one asks of the other
How are you making it with the itch?
Tra la ra la la la
Tra la ra la la la

******

It seems that in northern Mexico and southern New Mexico, there was an epidemic of a relatively harmless malady called "maguana", a sort of skin irritation that, though it did not break out like other similar irritations, had a very itchy sensation. Whenever an epidemic of any sort breaks out, the popular lyre takes it up. During some of the small pox epidemics of the last century a number of ballads were written in memory of a disastrous event. "La Maguana", however, not being very serious, was treated in this song in a somewhat humorous vein.

EL AMOR DE LAS MUJERES

El amor de las mujeres
Es como el de las gallinas
Que en faltandoles el gallo
A cualquier pollo se le arriman.

Qui qui re qui ri qui qui
Canta el gallito
Por eso lo quiero tanto
Por borrachito.

EL AMOR DE LAS MUJERES
  (The Love of Women)

The love of women
Is like that of the hens
Who when the rooster is not (with them
                            (at home
They go around with any young chick

Qui, qui, re, qui, ri, qui, qui,
Sings the little rooster
That's why I like him so much
Because he is a little tippler.

****

For a humorous effect, the popular bard
resorts to a comparison between women,
the indiscriminate fowl, and the household
cat. The object of such verses is obviously
that of clever entertainment, although there
is the traditional belief of inconstancy and
fickleness of women. This song is excepttionally well adapted to close harmony.

El Amor de las mujeres

EL BORRACHITO

Yo soy aquel borrachito
Que caramba, que caray!
Que cuando me ando pasiendo
Nomas un traguito tomo
Que caramba, que caray!
Y para andarlos tanteando
Ujala que me ladeo
Ya voy a dejar el vicio
Nomas un traguito tomo
Para no perder el juicio.

Yo soy aquel borrachito
Que caramba, que caray!
Que cuando ando en la alameda
Saco mi punta de espada
Que caramba que caray!
Y me rifo con cualquiera
Ujala que me ladeo
Ya voy a dejar el vicio
Nomas un traguito tomo
Para no perder el juicio.

EL BORRACHITO
(The Little Tippler)

I am that little tippler, Oh me! Oh my!
Who when I am taking a stroll,
I only take a little swig, Oh me! Oh my!
And so as to get their number
I'm hoping that I'll wobble
I am going to break the habit
Just a little swig I'll take
So as not to go mad.

I am that little tippler, Oh me! Oh my!
Who when I am in the poplar grove
I draw out my sword, Oh me! Oh my!
And I scuffle with anybody
I'm hoping that I'll wobble.
I am going to break the habit
Just a little swig I'll take
So as not to go mad.

****

A person who indulges in drinking is usually considered amusing, and his antics have been the subject of humorus treatment by a large number of songs under this same title. None of the songs are serious, and they are usually given to entertainment. When such songs are being sung by the trovador, there is usually a certain amount of pantomine that accompanies them.

EL DIA DE TU SANTO

    Dios bendiga este dia venturoso
    Y bendiga la prenda que adoro
    Ya los angeles cantan en coro
    Por los años que cumples mi bien.

    Las estrellas se visten de gala
    Y la luna se llena de encanto
    Al saber que hoy es dia de tu
          santo
    Por los años que cumples mi bien.

EL DIA DE TU SANTO
(Your Saint's Day)

God bless this happy day
And bless the loved one that I adore;
And may the angels sing in chorus
For the years that you have attained, my dear

The stars are in gala attire
And the moon is full of enchantment
In knowing that today is your saint's day
Because of the years that you have (reached,) my dear.
                      (completed)

****

It was customary of the Spanish population
in New Mexico to greet a person upon his
birthday with some appropriate song. This
song is more on the order of a blessing and
could almost be considered a religious song.
It is best known in the southern part of the
state, where Mrs. Albert J. Fountain, of old
Mesilla, sang it on her seventy-fifty birthday.

LAS CAMPANAS DE BELEN

Son las dos y todos duermen
   en silencio
Solo se oyen las campanas
   de Belen
Donde se encuentra un pobresito
   prisionero
Por el amor y la traicion de
   una mujer
Por la amor y la traicion de
   una mujer.

Yo les digo a mis amigos que
   no sufran
Ni se crean del amor de una
   mujer
Por que el amor de las mujeres
   es muy grande
Y nos conduce a un eterno
   padecer.

LAS CAMPANAS DE BELEN
(The Bells of Bethlehem)

It is two o'clock and
everybody sleeps in silence;
The bells of Bethlehem can be heard
Where one finds a poor little prisoner
Because of his love for and the treason
of a woman,
Because of his love for and the treason
of a woman.

****

At first glance this song would appear to
be a religious song, but it is, in reality,
the plaintive wailing of a prisoner who
can hear the bells ringing as he lies
in prison as the result of a woman. The
song may have been composed in the village
of Belen, in central New Mexico, but it is
strange that the composition is known in
the northern part, where it was recorded
from a young trovador, Salamon Garcia, from
Arroyo Hondo.

ME CASÉ CON UNA POCHA

    Me Casé con una pocha
    Para aprender Ingles
    Y a los tres dias de casados
    Yo ya le decia "yes"

    Las pochas de California
    No saben comer tortilla
    No saben comer tortilla
    Por que solo en su casa
    Comen pan con mantequilla.

ME CASE CON UNA POCHA
  (I married a Pocha)

I married a pocha
So as to learn English
And after three days of married life
I already said "yes" to her.

The pochas from California do not
know how to eat "tortillas"
Because in their homes they only
use bread with butter.

    ****

The word "Pocha" literally means "discolored",
but in the Southwest and in Mexico it means "bob-
tailed". This is the nick-name given to the
Californians who are chided for their inability
to speak Spanish correctly. The entire song is
a mild and humorous criticism of the ways of a
"Pocha". There are several songs of this
nature and often the same words may be sung to
different tunes.

Me Casé Con Una Pocha

CHAPARRITA

Que bonitos ojos tienes chaparrita
No los vayas a tirar a la desgracia
Chaparrita no me quieren en tu casa
Dame tu mano para decirte adios.

En tu casa me han privado de que te ame
En tu casa ni uno de ellos puede ver me
Chaparrita no me dejes de querer
Dame tu mano para decirte adios.

Ya te he dicho ya no quiero
Y; ay no puedo
Vivir lejos y ausente de tus miradas
Mejor quiero verte muerta a punaladas
Antes que verte en brazos
De otro amor.

Chaparrita

What beautiful eyes you have Chaparrita,
Don't cast them to disgrace.
Chaparrita they don't like me in your home,
Give me your hand to bid you Good-Bye.

2

In your home they have forbidden me to love you;
In your home not even one of them can see me.
Chaparrita never stop loving me:
Give me your hand to bid you Good-Bye.

CHAPARRITA

If a girl were called "Shorty" in English she would not take it as an amorous appellation. In Spanish, "Chaparrita" is a diminutive that carries with it a certain connotation favorable and personal. Because there are so many small women in Hispanic countries. The men like to sing to them. Traditionally, however, the petite type is much attractive to Spaniards.

SOÑANDO

Soñando, soñando paso las horas morena
tus ojos tan bellos
Que quiero verte a mi lado
voy a comprarte un rebocito
Que quiero verte cerca de mi
Por que mis penas no tienen calma
Desde el momento en que yo te vi

Morena, morena supieras cuanto te quiero
Por que eres, porque eres
De mi alma el amor primero
Con tus ojitos me vuelves loco
Y quitas mi alma de padecer
Y si prometes serme constante
Tuyo mi amor siempre ha de ser

SOÑANDO
(Dreaming)

Dreaming, dreaming I spend the hours, brunette
Your eyes so pretty
That I want to see you by my side
I am going to buy you a little shawl
For I want to see you close to me
Because my griefs have no relief
Since the moment that I saw you.

Brunette, brunette, if you only knew how much
I love you
Because you are, because you are
The first love of my soul
With your little eyes you turn me mad,
and free my soul from suffering
And if you promise to be true to me
Yours, my love will always be.

****

ANNOTATION

The dreamy lover sings loudly of all the nice
things that he would like to do for his love.
This highly imaginative type of romance has a
great recurrence in the New Mexico repertoire.
A large number of folk songs go by that name,
but they are unrelated except in name.

EL LIRIO

Hay un lirio que el tiempo lo
        consume
Y hay una fuente que lo hace
        enverdecer
Hay un lirio que el tiempo lo
        consume
Y hay una fuente que lo hace
        enverdecer
Tu eres el lirio y dame tu
        perfume
Yo soy la fuente y dejame
        correr
Tu eres el lirio y dame tu
        perfume
Yo soy la fuente y dejame
        correr

EL LIRIO
(The Lily)

There is a lily that ages with time
There is a fountain that makes it grow green
There is a lily that ages with time
There is a fountain that makes it grow green
You are the lily, give me your perfume;
I am the fountain, let me keep on flowing.
You are the lily, give me your perfume
I am the fountain, let me keep on flowing.

****

Other comparisons, such as the one appearing in "The Love of Women", are not as complimentary as the comparison made in this particular song. The figure of speech is a favorite method of expression of the folk. The metaphor and the simile in particular have been popular with the trovador. "El Lirio" is known throughout the Southwest because it has such an easy, natural harmony. Since a large number of the singers like to have someone who will sing alto, these songs that lend themselves easily to close harmony have had a wide diffusion.

El Lirio

Arr. by A. Armendariz

LA LADERA

Hay al pie de la ladera
Una casita azulita
Hay al pie de la ladera
Una muchacha bonita
Con jardin y enredadera
Que se llama la Rosita
Que en la tarde alli me espera
Pa decirme una cosita.

Vuela vuela pajarito
Vuela a donde esta Rosita
Vuela vuela pajarito
Vuela a donde esta Rosita
Anda dile que me espere
En la ventana chiquita
Anda dile que me espere
Pa besarle la boquita.

Por el puente del arco iris
Por el puente del arco iris
Anda un gavilan volando
Si tu mama le prohibe
Y me manda me retire
Lograra que no te mire
Pero quete olvide cuando.

LA LADERA
(The Mountain Slope)

There is at the foot of the slope
A little blue house
There is at the foot of the slope
A pretty girl;
With a garden and entwining vines
Whose name is Rosita
In the evening there she waits for me
To tell me

Fly, fly away little bird
Fly away to where Rosita is
Fly, fly away little bird
Fly away to where Rosita is
Go and tell her to wait for me
By the little window
Go and tell her to wait for me
So as to kiss her little mouth

By the rainbow's bridge
By the rainbow's bridge
A hawk is flying
If your mother forbids it,
And asks me to go away
She will succeed in keeping me from seeing you
But in forgetting you, Never.

****

It is not unusual to have such a name for this song since it is sung in a village that lies on a mountain slope. The bird messenger is again characteristic of the Spanish folk song. A number of ballads with this theme may be found in tradition.*

*Vide A. L. Campa, "Spanish Folksong in the Southwest", page 27.

EL DOMINGO LA CONOCI

El Domingo la conoci
Y el lunes la platicamos
El martes la fui a pedir
Y el miercoles nos casamos
El juebes nos enejamos
Y el viernes le di unos palos
El Sabado se murio
Y el domingo la enterramos
Despues que paso el entierro
Me fui para la plaza
Encuentrome con mi suegra
Y acabole con la Raza

EL DOMINGO LA CONOCI
(I met her on Sunday)

On Sunday I met her
We talked it over on Monday
On Tuesday I went to ask for her hand
And on Wednesday we were married
On Thursday we quarreled
And I beat her up on Friday
She died on Saturday
And on Sunday we buried her
After the burial was over
I went to town
Met up with my mother-in-law
And finished up with the family.

****

The melody of this song is almost identical with that of "Redwing". It tells of a young man who had met a girl on Sunday, courted her, married her, had a fight with her, and killed her, all in a week. Then, for good measure, he met her folks and got them out of the way, too. Were it not for the light treatment of the subject, it would almost be considered a very bloody song, which, of course, it isn't.

CORRIDO DEL INDIO VICTORIO

Dos años antes de ochenta
Este Indio se pronuncio
Varias victimas dejo
Y tambien viudas llorando.

En el Pueblo del Colorado
Todavia se estan acordando
Que otro Indio les hara mal
Por que yo Victorio cuando.

Cuando Terrazas salio
A acompanar a Victorio
Con mata Ortiz se encontro
Y acordaron en su bando.

Ya no andaras asustando
Ni a los correos matando
Te veran tus companeros
Victorio quien sabe cuando.

Ya no te valen trincheras
pá que te andes escapando
Si no son buenos rifleros
Y el que los anda mandando.

En el cerro de tres Castillos
Fue donde peleo Victorio
Este brinco peor que un grillo
Pero no hubo escapatorio.

CORRIDO DEL INDIO VICTORIO
(Ballad of the Indian Victorio)

Two years come eighty
This Indian rebelled
Several victims he left
And also widows weeping.

In Colorado's Pueblo
They are still remembering
That another Indian will wrong them
But Victorio never more.

No more will you go about surprising
Nor killing the mail men
Your companions will see you Victorio
But who knows when

No more will entrenchments serve you
By which you can escape
If they are not good riflemen
And he who directs them
In the hills of Tres Castillos
Is where Victorio fought
He jumped more than a cricket
But there was no escaping.

******

The famous Apache Indian chieftain, Victorio was particularly well known in the southern part of New Mexico, where he committed a number of depredations. In this ballad are told a number of his "achievements" in the year of 1878. The corrido is a modern development of the 16th century ballad and it is usually a narrative poem dealing with some heroic theme, preferably with some well known person as the center of interest.

RECUERDOS DE UNA INGRATA

Recuerdos de una ingrata
Que yo en un tiempo amaba
Y ahora mi orgullo sirve
De no volverle a hablar;
Mis ojos competian
Sus lagrimas por ella
Su amor como una estrella
Yo ya no vi brillar.

Yo sufro por querete
Y padesco por amarte
Y quisiera envenenarte
Con liquidos de amor
Seha de llegar el dia
En que tu martirio llegue
Y entonces ya no pueda
De tu ilusion gozar.

      Recuerdos de Una Ingrata
      (Remembrance of an Ungrateful)

           1
Remembrance from an ungrateful
That I at one time adored,
And now my pride serves
Not to even talk to you.
My eyes competed their tears for her,
Her love like a star
I no longer saw glitter.

           2
I grieve for you dear,
I grieve for your love.
I would like to poison you
With liquids of love.
The day will soon come
In which your torture will come;
Then I shall no longer
Your illusion enjoy.

           3
The birds no longer sing,
The flowers no longer have fragrance,
The stars no longer shine,
Every thing is gloomy.
The day will soon come
In which your torture will come,
Then I shall no longer
Your illusion enjoy.

RECUERDOS DE UNA INGRATA

Songs such as this one remind one of the fellow who wrote once:
    "Every night I rember how glad I am I have
    forgotten you".
The young lover seems to find a certain consolation in having forgotten his girl, but he still sings to her.

SON TRES FLORES

Son tres flores que corte por la manana
Y una de ellas tenia el boton delicioso
Yo la adore como al angel mas hermoso
Vivo triste apasionado de su amor.

Ya te he dicho que no quiero y ay no puedo,
Vivir lejos y ausente de tus miradas
Mejor quiero verte muerta a punaladas
Antes que verte en los brazos de otro amor.

Son Tres Flores
(They Are Three Flowers)

1

They were three flowers that I plucked this morning.
One of them had a beautiful bud.
I adored it like an angel most beautiful;
I live sadly passionate for her love.

2

I have told you that I do not want! Oh! I can't
Live without you; far away from you.
I would rather see you dead and stabbed
Before seeing you in the arms of another love.

SON TRES FLORES

There is a pagan strain in many Spanish songs -- lovers "adore" with the same casual air that they sing. A number of exaggerated figures of speech cause the lady to become an "angel", a brilliant star or a Goddess.

At times the songs are so subjective and personal that one must guess who the three flowers are in this song.

Spanish American Folk Songs of New Mexico, 1936–37, Unit No. 2

TABLE OF CONTENTS

La Fresca Rosa	- "The Fresh Rose"
La Gota	- "The Dewdrop"
No Me Mires	- "Do Not Look At Me"
Paso del Norte (Corrido)	- "Ballad of El Paso"
El Ruego	- "The Entreaty"
Gacela	- "The Doe"
Las Tardes del Invierno	- "Winter Evenings"
El Pajarillo Errante	- "The Errant Bird"
La Noche Esta Serena	- "The Night is Serene"
La Casita en el Cerrito	- "The Little House in the Mountain"
El Puñal	- "The Dagger"
Valse Apasionado	- "The Passionate Waltz"
En una Tarde Te Vi	- "One Evening I saw You"
El Corrido de Jose Elizoido	- "Ballad of Jose Elizoido"
Los Pollos de la Capital	- "The Chickens from the Capitol"
Decima del Sombrero de Petate	- "The Grass Hat"
A la Puerta del Cielo	- "At the Gate of Heaven"
Chimayó	- "Chimayo"

LA FRESCA ROSA

Yo vi una fresca rosa una manana
Perfumada y graciosa fresca y lozana
Que bella estaba; que bella estaba
Sobre su verde tallo se balanceaba;
se balanceaba

Y al reclinar la tarde la vi ya muerta
Perdida su fragancia y vida yerta
Soplo la brisa; soplo la brisa
Sus hojas se esparcieron como ceniza;
como ceniza

Asi pasan en la vida las ilusiones
El amor y los placeres y las pasiones
Se acaba todo; todo se acaba
Y en esta triste vida se acaba todo;
todo se acaba

La Fresca Rosa
(The Fresh Rose)

I saw a fresh rose one early morning
Fresh and gracious, pure and exuberant
It was beautiful, Oh! So beautiful
And on its green stem it swayed and swayed

And the ardent rays of the noon sun
Quickly wilted its exuberance
It was beautiful Oh! so beautiful
And on its green stem it swayed and swayed

And by dusk, I saw it dead
Its fragrance gone and its life still
A light breeze puffed, a light breeze puffed
And its leaves scattered, like ashes like ashes

And so life, illusions, love, pleasure and passions
Fade in this world and everything ends.
Everything ends in this sad world.
Everything ends in this sad world.

Note: – This song was sung by Mrs. Albert J. Fountain Sr. of Mesilla, New Mexico who is 75 years of age. It was handed down to her by her mother. This beautiful song well expresses the thought that life is like a fume that fades away, no matter how young and beautiful you may be, when you are touched by death, you too can be as cold and still as death itself.

La Gota

Al separarnos mi llanto brota
Como la gota sobre la flor
Y vierte mi alma tristes suspiros
Con los delirios de mi pasion

Y cuando me halle de ti distante
Ni un solo instante te olvidare
Y si no me amas Oh dura suerte
Hasta la muerte te olvidare

La Gota
(The Dewdrop)

At our parting a flood of tears bursts
As a dewdrop over the flower
And in my soul it empties
Sorrowful sighs with the illusion of my passion

And when from thee I am far away
Not for an instant shall I forget you
And if I am forsake, Oh! my misfortune
Until death will I forget you

This is a farewell song. In those days the people were very emotional, they would write a poem or compose a song to fit every occasion.

No Me Mires

No me mires por Dios te lo ruego
Ni recuerdes que yo fui tu amada
Por desgracia me encuentro casada
Con un hombre que nunca lo ame

Es verdad es verdad que esta vida
Se la tengo entregada a mi esposo
Y el sin duda se encuentra celoso
Porque a otro hombre yo quise adorar

Y si quieres seremos hermanos
Mientras pasa la vida en el mundo
Y entonces alla en el cielo
Libres pues nos podremos amar

(No Me Mire)
(Do Not Look At Me)

Don't look at me of thee I entreat
And forget that I was ever your lover
Unfortunately today I am married
To a man that I never adored.

2

It is true, It is true that my life
And my love has been pledged to my husband
And he no doubt feels jealous
For the love that I had for another

3

If you wish our love shall be brotherly
During our life time on earth
And in heaven afterwards
Free we shall love again

4

It is true, It is true and I am sorry
And I curse my unfortunate fate
I only wish that soon death may come
For my rest and eternal repose

******

Note; In the old days marriages were arranged between the parents of the boy and girl without their consent, and many times not knowing each other until the day of the wedding. This caused many unhappy marriages and undoubtedly the inspiration for this song.

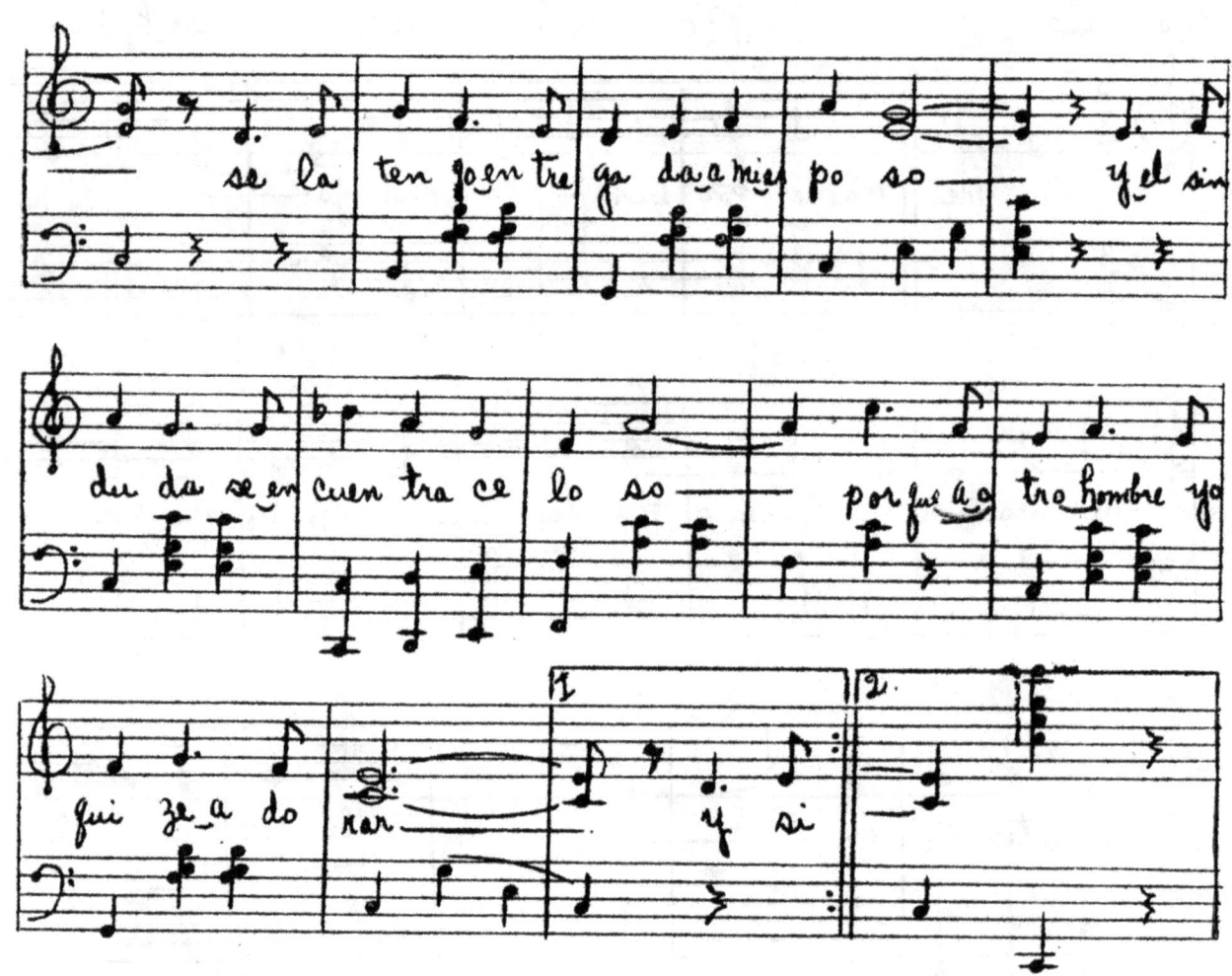

PASO DEL NORTE
(Corrido)

Paso del Norte que lejos te vas quedando
Puerto lucido de ti me voy aucentando;
Alla mis padres de mi se estan acordando
Solo Dios sabe si averlos yo volvere.

Ay que trabajos pasa el hombre ausente
Cuando anda aucente de su familia y su patria;
Pega un suspiro por su familia y por su chata,
Poco le falta para sentarse a llorar.

A que bonito es el Puerto de Mazatlan
Chulas sus calles, tambien su lucida plaza;
Pero mas bonito es el paseo en las olas altas,
Las que dirijen el buque en el ancho mar.

Paso Del Norte

Paso del Norte how far behind you are remaining
Of you gay Port I am going to depart
There my parents will be thinking of me
And God only knows if I shall ever see them again.

2

What hardships men go through when he is away from home
When he is away from his family and country
He sighs for his family, and longs to see his sweetheart
And he is not far from sitting and crying.

3

How beautiful is the Port of Mazatlan
The streets are beautiful, and the villego is gay
But more beautiful is to sail in the high waves
The waves that lead the boat in the wide sea.

****

Note: This song was composed by the settlers when they left Juarez in 1840. It seemed to them that they were leaving their families and homeland so very far behind, as traveling was so slow, some walked others rode burros. It took them a long time to get here because some traveled only at night as they were afraid the Indians might see them in the daytime. When they felt safe from the Indians they would sit around the camp fires and sing. This song was found and recorded at Dona Ana, New Mexico. It was sung by Mr. and Mrs Ledesma from that town.

Paso del Norte (corrido)

EL RUEGO

Ya no quiero que seas tan ingrata
Ni de angustias me dejes morir
Cuando sabes que tu eres mi vida
Y que muero de amores por ti

Aunque nunca tus labios pronuncien
Las palabras que ansioso perdi
Con tus ojos divinos y nobles
Con tus ojos contestame si

Si no quieres que te hable de amores
Has resuelto que muera infeliz
Si hay un ser que te impide quererme
Maldicion maldicion para mi

Si mi vida no fuera bastante
Para hacer a la tuya feliz
Otra vida yo al cielo pidiera
Y las dos las daria por ti

El Ruego
(The Entreat)

Don't look at me of thee I entreat
And forget that I was ever your lover
Unfortunately today I am married
to a man that I never adored

It is true It is true that my life
And my love has been pledged to my husband
And he no doubt feels jealous
For the love that I had for another

If you wish our love shall be brotherly
During our life time on earth
And in heaven afterwards
Free we shall love again

It is true It is true and I am sorry
And I curse my unfortunate fate
I only wish that soon death may come
For my rest and eternal repose

Note: — In the old days marriages were arranged between the parents of the boy and girl without their consent, and many times not knowing each other until the day of the wedding. This caused many unhappy marriages and undoubtedly the inspiration for this song.

Gacela

Ven Gacela, ven Gacela
Vente con migo al mar
Mira que quero ensenarte
Que aprendas a bogar

Sientate aqui, donde te pueda mirar
Donde tus ojos mi bien
Los pueda yo contemplar,
Que no mirandote asi
Voy a perder la razon
Pues arde en fuego voraz
Mi corazon

Gacela

Come Gacela, Come Gacela
Come with me to the sea
Listen, I want to teach you
How to row a boat

Sit here before me, where I can admire you
Where I can contemplate your beautiful eyes.
For not seeing you, I shall go mad
Because there is a constant flame in my
heart for you.

Note: - Gacela is a love song. It was sung by Mrs. Clotilde N. Armendariz from Mesilla, New Mexico, Mrs. Armendariz is 70 years of age, she used to sing this song when she was a child. She learned it from her mother.

Las tardes del invierno

En las tardes sombrias del invierno
Bajo un prado a llorar me reclino
Maldiciendo mi infausto destino
Que me cansa y me pesa el vivir

En las horas cansadas de estio
Bajo un prado me siento lloroso
Y alli exalo suspiro quejoso
No hay quien tenga compasion de mi

Por doquiera que miran mis ojos
No he podido encontrar la ventura
Solamente una fuerte amargura
He podido en la vida encontrar

Las Tardes Sombrias del Invierno
(The Gloomy Evenings of Winter)

In the gloomy evenings of winter
Under a meadow I lean back to cry
Cursing my unfortunate fate
That it wearies and grieves me to live

In the tiresome hours of summer
Under a meadow I sit down to weep
And there I exalt a plaintful sigh
There is no one to take pity on me

I have looked everywhere
And I cannot find my happiness
Only bitterness and contempt
Has my life been able to find

I don't want a feign love
I only wish for a true friend
To tell me in my weary hours
"At Your side I shall happy live".

Note: - This song was sung by Mrs. Albert J. Fountain Sr. of Mesilla, New Mexico. While the song has a beautiful melody it must have been composed by a very depressed or melancholic person who couldn't see the bright side of life, and it compared his whole miserable life with the gloomy evenings of winter. The song must be about 70 years old.

EL PAJARILLO ERRANTE

Soy pajarillo errante
Que ando vagando en pos de un nido,
Paso por la enrramada buscando abrigo
Buscando abrigo
Algo mi canto entre todas las aves
Y el que escucha no sabe que sufro tanto.

Cuando el cazador me busca por mi guarida,
Por mi guarida,
Defenderme no puedo tuya es mi vida,
Tuya es mi vida;
Also mi vuelo y me traicionan mis alas
Me traicionan mis alas volar no puedo.

Soy como el arroyuelo que siempre brota
Que siempre brota,
Por donde quiera que ando dejo una gota
Dejo una gota;
Pues mi destino es dejar gota por gota
Gotas de lagrimas por mi camino.

The Errant Bird

I am a wandering bird
I am looking for a nest
I wander through the branches looking for shelter,
Looking for shelter.
I raise my song among the birds
And the one who listens does not know that I grieve.

2

When the hunter seeks me, for my protection
For my protection.
I cannot defend myself, yours is my life.
Yours is my life.
I raise my flight and my wings betray me.
My wings betray me, I cannot fly.

3

I am like the brook for ever gushing
For ever gushing
Where ever I go I leave a drop, I leave a drop.
As my fate is to leave drop by drop
Tear drops all along my way.

******

Note: In this love song the author compares his
sad life with that of an errant bird. Dona Nestora
Mendoza de Lara from Lincoln, New Mexico who is
72 years of age used to sing all these love songs
at the dances to entertain the people.

LA NOCHE ESTA SERENA

La noche esta serena
Todo en silencio esta
Solo la luna palida
Es la que alumbra ya

Ven, que conmigo no habra tempestad
Mi barquilla es de flores
Sus remos de cristal
Solo la luna palida
El resplendor sera

La Noche Esta Serena
(The Night is Serene)

1

The night is serene
Everything is silent
Except the pale moon
That is illuming us.

2

Come with me there shall be no storm
My little boat is made of flowers
Its paddles are of crystal
And from the pale moon the splendor shall be.

La Noche esta Serena is a love song.
It was sung by Mr. A. J. Fountain, Sr.,
who is 75 years of age. He learned this
song when he was a very small boy. It
was used by the romantic trovadors to
serenade their sweethearts.

LA CASITA EN EL CERRITO

Donde estan aquellas horas
Que pasabamos tu y yo
Los dos bajo aquel techito
Nuestro amor nuestra ilusion;
Donde estan aquellas flores
El cantar del ruiseñor
Con sus cadencias de amores
Nos llenaba de pasion.

La casita, en el cerrito
Donde yo te conoci
Donde canta el pajarito
Primer beso que te di,
Las violetas, aquel mirto
Y las flores carmesi
Ven, vamos a aquel ranchito
Para estar junto de ti.

La Casita En El Cerrito
(The Little House in The Mountain)

Where are those hours
That you and I passed together
The two of us under that roof
Our love our illusion;
Where are those flowers
The song of the mocking-bird
With its love cadences
Would fill us with passion.

2

The little house in the mountain
Where I met you
Where the little bird sings
The first kiss that I gave you,
The violets, the myrtle
And the red flowers
Come, let us go to that little ranch
So that I may be near you.

****

Note: This song is beautiful in melody and rhythm, it's a song about a lover who is recalling all the beautiful things around the little house in the mountain that made his life happy together with his loved one. This song was recorded in Taos, New Mexico, where it is still sung by the Taos Quartet.

El Puñal

Toma mi vida el puñal y traspasa
Este pecho que amaste primero
Tu bien sabes que te amo y te quiero
Y por ti yo sere infelez.

2

Bajare silencioso a la tumba
A buscar mi perdido sosiego,
De rodillas ingrata te ruego
Que un momento te acuerdes de mi.

El Puñal
(The Dagger)
I

Take my love the dagger and trespass
This heart which once you loved
You well know that I love and adore you
And for you my happiness will be sacrificed.

2

Silently I shall decend to my tomb
In search of my lost love
On my knees I beg of you ungrateful
For a moment, to think of me.

Note: El Puñal is a love song. It was sung by Mrs. Campa, Dr. Arthur Campa's mother.

VALSE APASIONADO

Este es el valse apasionado
Por que tiene versos de pura pasion
Y como estaba entusiasmado
No sabia de su corazon.

No me desprecies no seas ingrata
No me desprecies, ten compasion de mi,
Mi corazon esta hecho pedazos
No sabe de su porvenir.

Este es el valse de un trovador
Que era un joben de poco vivir
Y como estaba entusiasmado
No sabia de su porvenir.

The Passionate Waltz

This is the passionate waltz
Because it has passionate words
And as he was in love
He did not know about his heart.

2

Do not scorn me, don't be ungrateful
Do not scorn me, take compassion of me
My heart is torn to pieces
It does not know of its future.

3

This is the waltz of a Trovador
An unexperienced young man
And as he was in love
He did not know of his future.

****

Note: The stanzas in this song tell of a young
Trovador who was so very much in love that he
disregarded his own life and future. This song was
found in Lincoln New Mexico. Dona Nestora Mendoza de Lara
who is now 72 years of age and who in the olden days
was a very noted singer, used to sing these old love
songs at the dances and receptions, as it was customary
to engage a Poet or a Singer to entertain at the dances.

EN UNA TARDE TE VI

En una tarde te vi joven querida
Virgen de amor
Tan solo mi amor rendido
Por que eres mi adoracion

Mira mi alma cuanto sufro por ti
Si tu me amas te amare con frenesi
Si me quieres que feliz sere yo
De un encanto me servira tu amor.

One Evening I Saw You

One evening I saw you dear Maiden
Oh! Virgen of love
And I rendered my love to you
Because you are my adoration.

2

Oh! my soul, how I suffer for you
If you love me, I shall love you with frenzy.
If you love me, how happy I shall be
And I shall be charmed with your love

Note: This song was very popular in the year 1879. It was recorded by Mr. Amador Avalos in Tularosa, New Mexico.

CORRIDO DE JOSE ELIZOIDO

Domingo por cierto fué
Cuando el caso susedió
Que el pobre Jose Elisoido
A su madre le falto.

Su madre como enojada
Una maldicion le hechó
A los pies de su Santo Cristo
Que hasta la tierra tembló.

Le pido a Dios hijo mio
Le pido a todos los Santos
Que te haz de caer de la mina
Y hacerte dos mil pedasos.

Por Dios madrecita mia
Que dice su corazon
Soy hijo de sus entrañas
Nacido del corazon.

Por Dios madrecita amada
Levante su maldicion
Soy hijo de sus entrañas
Querido del corazon.

El lunes por cierto fué
Que a la mina se acercó
Y le dice a su minero
No quisiera bajar yo.

Y le dice su minero
Por que no quieres bajar?
Anda y vuelvete aprisa
Busca quien baje en tu lugar.

De alli se volvió Jose
Y pensando a quien allar
Sus amigos se negaron
El se volvió a su lugar.

Enciendanse pues las velas
Pa comensar a bajar
Que el pobre Jose Elisoido
Su muerte vino a buscar.

Tomó el primer escalón
Y luego se encomendó
Al Señor Sacramentado
Y a la cruz donde murió.

Tomó el segundo escalón
Y luego se despidió
La compañia que llevava
En un paño lo sacó.

Los sesos los pepenaron
En la copa de un sombrero
Esto es para enblandecer
Los corazones de acero.

Adios todos mis amigos
Adios todita la gente
Pues este es el fin que tiene
Un hijo desobediente.

Ya con esta me despido
De las hojas del Manzano
Este caso susedió
El dia veintidos de Mayo.

Ya con esta me despido
De todos los que me han oido
Estas son las mañanitas
Del pobre Jose Elisoido.

CORRIDO OF JOSE ELIZOIDO

It was on Sunday
When the event occured
That poor Jose Elizoido
Beat up his mother

His fretful mother
Knelt at the feet of a Holy Christ
A curse cast upon him
That made the earth shake

I ask God my son
I ask all his Saints
That from the mine you shall fall
And that you be smashed into two thousand pieces

For God's sake my little mother
What does your heart speak?
I am your own blood
Born from thy heart

For God's sake my loved mother
Lift thy curse on me
I am your own son
Born from your heart

It was on Monday
To the mine he went
He tells the miner
That he would not like to go down the mine

His miner askes him
Why don't you want to go down the mine?
Go and come right back
Ask someone to go down in your place

From there Jose came back
Thinking who he would get to go down in his place
All his friends refused to go down
Then Jose took his place in the mine

Light up the candles
That I may start down the mine
Poor Jose Elisoido
His death came to find

He took his first step down
And then he began to pray
To the Holy Sacrament
And to the cross where he died

He took his second step down
And then he bid them all farewell
The ones that were in his company
Brought his flesh up in a handkerchief

His brains were gathered
In the cup of a hat
And this is to soften
The hearts of steel

Good-bye all my friends
Good-bye all the people
This is how the life ends
Of a disobedient son

With this I end my song
Bidding farewell to El Manzano   (The place where this
This event happened   happened)
The twenty second of May

With this I end my song
To all that have heard my song
This is the sad story
Of poor Jose Elizoido.

El Corrido De Jose Elizoido. A disobedient child was chastized severely in days gone by. When a son went to the extreme of beating his parents, a curse was cast upon him. The child then lived in fear of retribution for years afterward. The story of Jose Elizoido is supposed to have happened at El Manzano. The popular bard has simply set to music the incident in keeping with the folk balladry.

LOS POLLOS DE LA CAPITAL

Yo conosco ciertos pollos
De tan rara condicion
Que quieren hacer conquistas
Sin salir del cascarón
Cuando ven alguna polla
Que por la calle va
Abriendo las alitas
Le dicen ven acá.

Ellas los siguen con mucho afán
Dicen lo que sienten con barbaridad,
A la solitea y a la solita
Estos son los pollos de la Capital.

Tambien hay pollos chiquitos
Que les gusta en profesión
Con eso que son chiquitos
Les palpita el corazon;
Cuando ven una pollita
Que les hace qui, ri, qui qui..
Torsiendose—solitas
Les dicen si, si si..,

Ellas los siguen con mucho afán
Dicen lo que sufren con barbaridad
A-la-solitea y a la solita
Estos son los pollos de la Capital.

Tambien hay pollos chiquitos
Que le roban a su mamá
Pa regalar a la polla
Una conquista de a real,
Si tienen algun enojo
Les dicen sin vacilar
Devuelveme mis prendas
Que se enoja mi mama.
Ellas los siguen con mucho afan, etc..

Tambien hay gallinas viejas
Untadas de almidon
Con eso que son tan viejas
Les palpita el corazon,
Cuando ven algun gallote
Que les hace ca, ra, ca, ca.
Abriendo sus alotas
Les dicen ven acá

Ellas los siguen con mucho afan, etc.,

LOS POLLOS DE LA CAPITAL
(The Chickens from the Capital)

I know certain little chickens
Of a very rare type
That want to make love
And they are not even hatched
When they see a little chicken
That on the street goes by
Opening their little wings
They tell her "Come here"

    Chorus

They follow them with great care
What they feel, they very frankly tell
Shaking here and shaking there
These are the Chickens from the Capital

There are also little chickens
That make it their profession
With that, that they are so little
Their little heart pants
When they see a little chicken
Who sings to them Qui, ri qui, qui
Twisting up themselves
They say yes, yes, yes.

    Chorus

They follow them with great care
What they feel they very frankly tell
Shaking here and shaking there
These are the chickens from the Capital

There are also little chickens
That from their mothers still
To make a gift to their love
A love gift of a quarter
If they happen to break up
They tell them very frankly
Give me back my jewels
Because my mother gets angry

    Chorus

There are also old hens
Their faces white washed with starch
With that, that they are so old
Their old heart also pants
When they see a big old rooster
That sings to them Ca, ra, ca, ca!
Opening up their old big wings
They tell them "Come Here".

****

Los Pollos De La Capital is a good example of mild satire. The combination of humor and satire is characteristically Spanish. A large number of songs devote one or two stanzas to a fad, custom, or social condition. This one deals particularly with the presumptiousness of young people. This particular song is used as a dance tune as well.

DECIMA DEL SOMBRERO DE PETATE

Cuando andaba de pretendiente
Que andaba tan presumido
Compre una rica mantilla
Y mi sombrero de Petate

Compre una rica mantilla
Y un sombrero de petate
De cuero le hice toquilla
De barbiquejo un mecate
De las costras de un metate
Tendi una cama decente
En un lugar solamente
De los lugares mas finos
Dormia como los cochinos
Cuando andaba de pretendiente.

Compré una camisa blanca
Bien del color del venado
Pero no les cause risa
Que no me la habian lavado
Compre un chaleco nevado
Y de pelos enguarnecido
Compre un ceñidor podrido
Que un forastero me vendio
Yo no se que tenia yo
Que andaba tan presumido.

Una leva de cola
Tenia cuando era soltero
Tambien una leva muy fina
Que me halle en el basurero
Y tambien mucho dinero
Que en la memoria tenia
Pero nadie lo sabia,
Solamente yo, en mi intento
Y con mi loco pensamiento
Compré una rica mantilla.

Me senté junto a un rico
Y estaba muy bien peinado
Me quité mi sombrerito
Y le gané abatanado
Le puse muy bien cuidado
No me hablara un disparate
Y por interés me mate
Por que no le doy combate
Con mis chanclas arrastrando
Y mi sombrero de petate.

DECIMA OF THE PALM LEAF HAT

When I was a suitor
And I was so conceited
I bought a rich mantilla
And my palm leaf hat

I bought a rich mantilla
And a palm leaf hat
Out of hide I made a hat band
And a cord served as a guard ribbon
From the crusts of a metate*
I made me a decent bed
In one place only
Among the finest of all places
I used to sleep like the pigs
When I was a suitor

I bought a white cloth shirt
Much like the color of a deer
But do not laugh
As no one had washed it for me
I bought a vest white as snow
And trimmed with hair
I bought a rotted sash
Which a foreigner sold to me
I don't know what was the matter with me
That I was so conceited

I had a frock tail coat
When I was single
I also had a very fine coat
Which I found in the rubbish pile
I also had much money
In my memory
But no one knew about it
Only me, in my purpose
And with my crazy mind
I bought a rich mantilla

I sat closely to a wealthy man
And my hair was very nicely combed
I took my little hat off
And I beat him dressed
I watched him closely
Not to talk nonsense to me
And by inducement kill me
Because I could not give him battle
With my old shoes dragging
And my palm leaf hat

*Metate is a curved stone for grinding corn, maize.

※※※※※※※※※※※※※

Decima del Sombrero de Petate is a peculiar type of folk song that flourished in the first half of the 19th century in New Mexico. Although known in Cuba and South America it never gained the same popularity that it did in New Mexico. Metrically it is composed of 44 lines with an introductory quatrain and four ten-line stanzas. The tenth line of every stanza forms the introductory quatrain. Outside of the religious Alabado, the Decima has preserved more completely the qualities of Andalusian-Moorish music than any other form of folk song known in the Southwest. It was customary for the troubadour to recite the quatrain by way of introduction.

A LA PUERTA DEL CIELO
(cancion de cuna)

A la puerta del cielo
Venden zapatos
Para los angelitos
Que andan descalzos
Duermete niño, Duermete niño
A rru, a ruu.

****

This is a Lullaby, sung by Miss Anita Bergere in Santa Fe, New Mexico. It is uded as a cradle song to rock children to sleep.

AT THE GATE OF HEAVEN

At the gate of Heaven
They sell shoes
For the little angels
Who go barefooted,
Sleep baby, sleep baby
Rock-a-bye, rock-a-bye.

"Chimayó."

Arr. by A. Armendariz

Annotation to Chimayo

Chimayó is an old waltz. It was recorded in Taos New Mexico from an old musician. In the olden days the people used to dance a waltz in many ways; Chimayó is a Vals Redondo meaning in English (A Round Waltz) which is danced to music that is quick and lively as you will notice in the Chimayo music. This waltz was composed in honor of Chimayó, New Mexico, a town in the northern part of the State.

Spanish American Singing Games of New Mexico, Revised 1940, Unit No. 3

COMPILED BY WORKERS OF THE

WORK PROJECTS ADMINISTRATION

of

New Mexico

FEDERAL WORKS AGENCY

John M. Carmody, Administrator

WORK PROJECTS ADMINISTRATION

F. C. Harrington, Commissioner
Florence Kerr, Assistant Commissioner
James J. Connelly, State Administrator

FOREWORD

This collection is designed for use by teachers and others who work with children. It is hoped that its use will encourage the collection of other singing games and that both Spanish and English versions will be sung. Originally in Spanish, the songs have been translated freely into English so that the English would be singable even though the translations were not literal. These games have been sung and played in New Mexico for generations and are still in use.

The book is a collaboration of workers on the New Mexico Music Project, under the supervision of Helen Chandler Ryan, and the New Mexico Writers' Project, the first sponsored by the New Mexico State Department of Education and the second by the Coronado Cuarto Centennial Commission. In the table of contents, credit is given to the one who collected the song; but special acknowledgment is due the following: Aurelio Armendariz, who, in addition to collecting most of them, made the original arrangements and most of the transcriptions; Professor A. L. Campa, head of the folklore department of the University of New Mexico, who gave unstintingly of his time and rendered invaluable service in checking the manuscripts and establishing the authenticity of the games; Miss Marie Isabel Sena, of the faculty of the Santa Fe High School, who checked and read proof on the directions in Spanish; Anita Osuna Carr, who helped with the poetic translations; Charles M. Kinney, who assisted in the arrangement of the accompaniments; Messrs. Seeger, Botkin, and Royce, experts on folklore and consultants to the federal government at Washington, D. C., for their criticism and advice.

Piano accompaniments have been provided for the convenience of those who cannot dispense with either the piano or an accompaniment; but because of the folk quality of these songs it is hoped that if any instrumental accompaniment is used, it will be that of the village fiddle or guitar instead of the piano.

                         Charles Ethrige Minton
                         State Supervisor
                         New Mexico Writers' Project

TABLE OF CONTENTS

Naranja Dulce: Sweet Orange
    Aurelio Armendariz

Juan Pirulero: John Pirulero
    José Gonzalez and Aurelio Armendariz

María Blanca: Lovely Mary
    Aurelio Armendariz and José Gonzalez

Arre, Mi Burrito: Giddy-up, My Little Burro
    José Gonzalez

Doña Ana No Está Aquí: Lady Anne
    Amador Avalos and Aurelio Armendariz

Rueda de San Miguel: St. Michael's Wheel
    Aurelio Armendariz

La Tabla: The Table
    Aurelio Armendariz

Víbora de La Mar: Sea Serpent
    Aurelio Armendariz

El Florón: The Flower
    Aurelio Armendariz

Hilitos de Oro: Little Threads of Gold
    Aurelio Armendariz

La Viudita de Santa Isabel: The Widow of St. Isabel
    Aurelio Armendariz

La Huerfanita: The Little Orphan
    Aurelio Armendariz

Ambo Gato: Ambo Gato
    Aurelio Armendariz

NARANJA DULCE

Naranja dulce, limón, partido
Dame un abrazo por Dios te pido
Si fueran falsos mis juramentos,
En otros tiempos, se han de olvidar
Toca la marcha, mi pecho llora.
Adiós señora, ya yo me voy.

DIRECCIONES: Cuatro o más niños pueden jugar este juego. Para principiar uno de los niños es escogido y se para en el medio de un círculo formado por los otros niños cogidos de la mano. Mientras le rodean y cantan la Naranja Dulce el que está en el medio aguarda las palabras "dame un abrazo" y en seguida escoge uno de los niños y lo mete para el medio junto con él y le da un abrazo.

En seguida estos dos simulan o hacen las mociones como si estuviesen tocando un violín, una guitarra o cualquier otro instrumento que se les ocurra.

Al cantarse las últimas palabras, o donde dice "Adiós Señora, ya yo me voy," los dos niños en el medio se dan la mano y se despiden, el primero juntándose con los demás en el círculo. El segundo se queda en el círculo y el juego sigue adelante como descrito

SWEET ORANGE

An orange sweet and a lemon sour,
Give me a kiss, Dear, beneath this bower;
If I should fail, Dear, to keep my promise,
You would forget as once long ago.
I hear the music and feel like crying,
Goodbye, my lady, for I must go.

DIRECTIONS: The game is played by four or more children. The child who is chosen "it" stands in the center of a circle formed by the other children who hold hands and circle as they sing. At the words, "Give me a kiss," the child who is "it" chooses one from the circle and draws him or her into the center. The two children in the center then go through the motions of playing the violin, the guitar, or any other musical instrument. At the words, "Goodbye, my lady," the two children shake hands. The child who was kissed is now "it" and remains in the center of the circle, while the one who was "it" returns to the circle and joins with the other children, The same procedure is repeated for the duration of the game.

(If desired, "hug" may be sung instead of "kiss" and the action changed accordingly. In the Spanish, the word is "embrace")

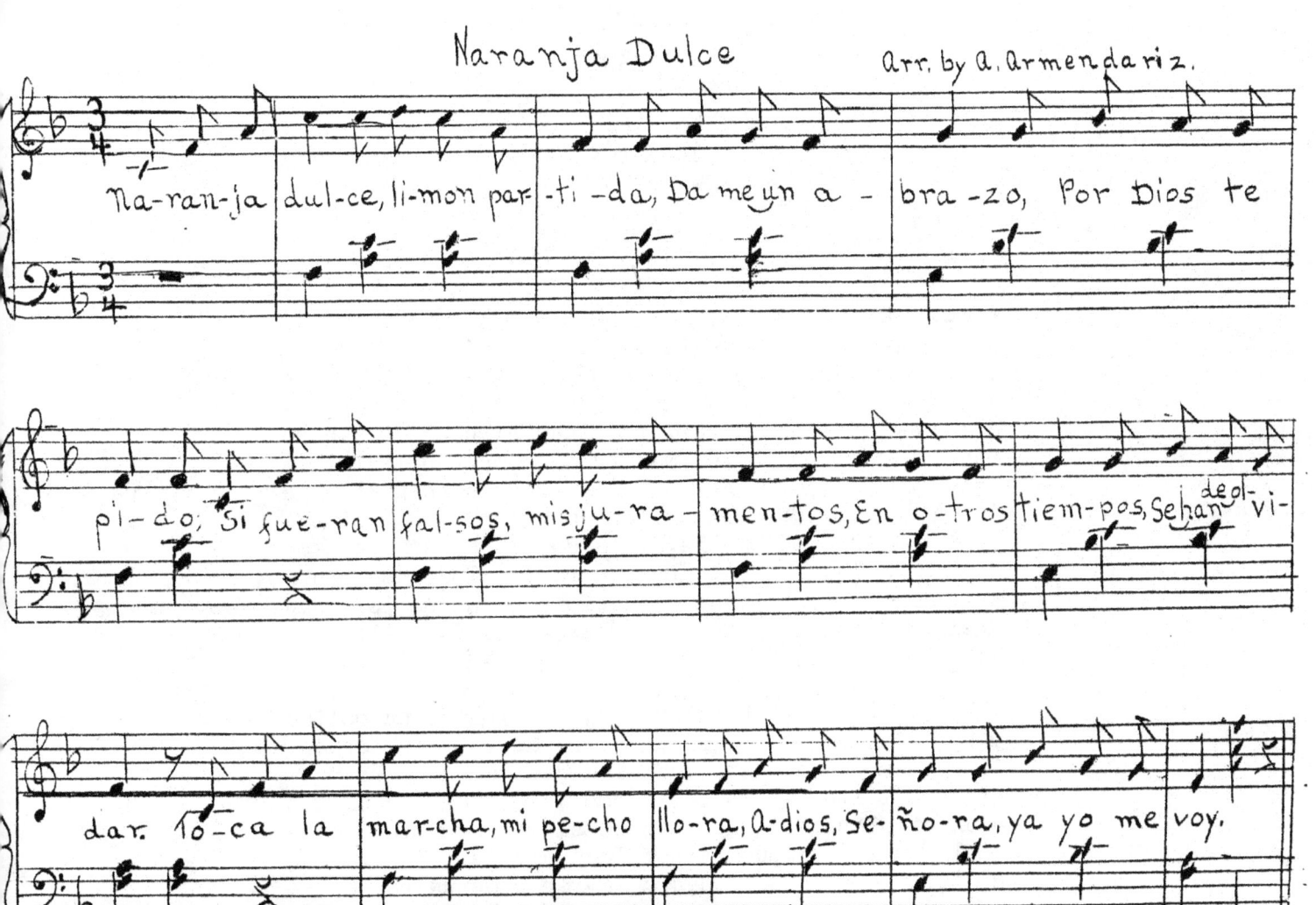

Naranja Dulce

Arr. by A. Armendariz.

Na-ran-ja dul-ce, li-mon par-ti-da, Da me un a-bra-zo, Por Dios te pi-do; Si fue-ran fal-sos, mis ju-ra-men-tos, En o-tros tiem-pos, Se han de ol-vi-dar. To-ca la mar-cha, mi pe-cho llo-ra, A-dios, Se-ño-ra, ya yo me voy.

JUAN PIRULERO

Este es el juego de Juan Pirulero
Que cada quien atiende a su juego.
Este es el juego de Juan Pirulero,
Que cada quien atiende a su juego.

DIRECCIONES: Un sinnúmero de niños pueden jugar este juego. Primero se escoge de entre ellos uno que sea Juan Pirulero. Después de ser escogido Juan Pirulero, él se para en el centro de los demás niños, sentados en el suelo. Juan Pirulero canta su canción continuamente mientras se da vueltas imitando un molino. Antes les ha dado a cada niño la tarea de imitar o hacer las mociones como si estuviesen partiendo leña, amasando, lavando ropa, tocando el violín o guitarra en fin. Todos se ponen a imitar las diferentes acciones que se les han designado mientras Juan Pirulero se da vueltas y sigue cantando.

De repente Juan Pirulero deja de imitar un molino y se pone a imitar algún otro de los muchachos. Este si no está descuidado inmediatamente debe ponerse a imitar el molino como lo estaba haciendo Juan Pirulero. Si no lo hace al momento tiene multa la cual es impuesta por Juan Pirulero y será que el delincuente se ponga a ladrar como un perro, se pare de cabeza, llore como un niño, o cualquier impuesto ridículo o divertido que se le ocurra a Juan Pirulero. Y así sigue el juego.

JOHN PIRULERO

This is the game of one John Pirulero,
Let all the players attend to their game.
This is the game of one John Pirulero,
Let all the players attend to their game.

DIRECTIONS: Any number of children may play this game. A leader, John Pirulero, is chosen. He stands in the center of a circle formed by the other children who sit cross-legged on the floor. John Pirulero sings the song and at the same time makes a circular motion in imitation of turning a grindstone. He then assigns to each child the task of sawing wood, kneading dough, playing the violin, washing clothes, and similar tasks, all of which they imitate with their arms and hands. John Pirulero now and then changes from grinding to the task of one of the players, and the player imitating the task must immediately change to the task of grinding corn. If the child happens to be caught napping and does not change to John Pirulero's task of grinding, he is given a sentence and must pay a penalty given by John Pirulero, such as howling like a dog, hopping on one foot, etc. The game continues indefinitely.

Juan Pirulero

Recorded by José Gonzalez.
Arr. by A. Armendariz.

És-te es el juego de Juan Pi-ru-le-ro,
Que cada quien a-tien-da a su jue-go.

MARÍA BLANCA

María Blanca está encerrada
En pilares de oro y plata.
Abriremos un pilar
Para ver a María Blanca.

DIRECCIONES: Un sinnúmero de niños pueden jugar este juego. Todos menos dos de ellos forman un círculo, cogidos de la mano. Uno de los dos es designado María Blanca y se queda adentro del círculo, el otro se queda afuera.

Los niños del círculo cantan las primeras dos líneas del verso arriba. El niño de afuera canta las últimas dos líneas mientras él o ella hace fuerza que se suelten de la mano, los niños del círculo, y así penetrar él adentro. Si logra hacerlo, María Blanca sale a huir.

Mientras el niño o la niña que ha rompido el círculo, sale en pos de María Blanca haciendo fuerza cogerla, los niños del círculo alzan las manos en alto así dándole oportunidad a María Blanca para entrar al círculo otra vez. Si ella logra entrar safa, sin ser cogida, el juego sigue adelante, pero si al contrario ella fuese prendida tiene que tomar el puesto afuera del círculo, uniendose el que la cogió con los del círculo y otra María Blanca es escogida.

LOVELY MARY

Lovely Mary is encircled
In a cell where she must tarry,
Let us break her silver prison
And set free our Lovely Mary.

DIRECTIONS: A number of small children play this game. All but two form a circle, holding hands; one child, designated as Lovely Mary, remains within the circle and the other, outside.

The children forming the circle sing the first two lines of the verse. The child outside the circle sings the last two lines as he or she tries to loosen the hands of the children forming the circle. If he is successful, Lovely Mary runs out.

While the child who has broken the circle runs after Lovely Mary, trying to catch her, the children forming the circle hold their hands high in the air thus giving her a chance to enter the circle again. If she returns to safety the game continues as before; but if she is caught she becomes the one outside the circle, her captor joins the circle, and a new Lovely Mary is chosen.

ARRE, MI BURRITO

Arre, mi burrito, que vamos a Belén
Que mañana es fiesta y el otro también
Arre, arre, lléveme usted al trote,
Arre, arre, arre, lléveme al galope
De prisa, de prisa.

DIRECCIONES: Los niños se forman en línea fingiendo ir montados en burro mientras cantan la canción arriba. Acabandose la canción ellos se paran poco lejos el uno del otro, con las manos puestas firmemente sobre los muslos un poco arriba de la rodilla, y con la cabeza agachada como si fuesen burritos.

El niño al pie de la línea corre y brinca sobre los demás, de uno en uno, hasta llegar a la cabeza de la línea donde se agacha como los demás. Luego el niño que queda al pie de la línea hace lo mismo, y así de uno en uno hasta que todos por su turno hayan brincado sobre los demás.

GIDDY-UP, MY LITTLE BURRO

Giddy-up, my burro, we're going to Belén,
Fiesta is tomorrow, and one next day again.
Hurry, hurry, hurry.....
Let us go a-pacing,
Hurry, hurry, hurry.....
Let us go a-racing.
O hurry....O hurry......

DIRECTIONS: The children form a line and go through the motions of riding a burro as they sing. When the song is ended the children stand some distance apart, placing their hands on their thighs, and keeping their heads bowed in imitation of a burro. The one last in line runs and leaps over each player in succession. When he has leaped over the last child, he in turn stoops at the head of the line, and the last player runs and leaps over the others until all have had a turn.

This game is similar to Leap Frog.

DOÑA ANA NO ESTÁ AQUÍ

Doña Ana no está aquí
Está en su vergel
Abriendo la rosa
Y cerrando el clavel

Vamos a dar la vuelta
Al toro toronjil
A ver a Doña Ana
Comiendo perejil

Quien es esta gente
Qué pasa por aquí
Que ni de día ni de noche
Me dejan dormir?

Somos los estudiantes
Que venimos a estudiar
A la capillita
De la virgen del pilar.

DIRECCIONES: Todos menos uno, de los niños participando en este juego, se forman en circulo y cantan los primeros dos versos de la canción arriba. La niña, designada Doña Ana se sienta en el centro y hace mociones en conformidad con las acciones mencionadas en los versos, uno y dos. Doña Ana canta el tercer verso mientras los niños dan vuelta al rededor de ella. Luego los niños cantan el último verso y acabándolo de cantar el juego sigue con el siguiente dialogo:

Los Niños:	Cómo está Doña Ana?
Doña Ana:	Tiene calentura.
Los Niños:	Cómo está Doña Ana?
Doña Ana:	Está muriendose.
Los Niños:	Cómo está Doña Ana?
Doña Ana:	Está muerta.

Al contestar Doña Ana que está muerta se tiende en el suelo y los niños le rodean a ver si es cierto que está muerta. Entonces Doña Ana revive y brinca en pos de los niños, y ellos salen a huir. El niño o niña a quien ella logre coger será Doña Ana en la siguiente repitición del juego.

LADY ANNE

Where is the Lady Anne,
Within her garden wall...?
A rosebud she is opening,
And closing pinks so small.

Come let us go a-strolling,
Just to see what we can see,-
I think the Lady Anne,
Eats parsley by that tree.

Who can these people be,
Who pass my house like sheep?
All day and night they wander
And never let me sleep.

We are the famous students
Who have come to study here;
We come to see the chapel
Of the Virgin Mary dear.

DIRECTIONS: All but one of the children playing this game form a circle and sing the first two verses of the song. The child designated as Lady Anne sits in the center and goes through the motions indicated by the words in verses one and two. Lady Anne sings the third verse as the children walk around and around her. The children sing the fourth verse. When the singing is over, the following questions are asked and answered:

The Children:	How is Lady Anne?
Lady Anne:	She has a fever.
The Children:	How is Lady Anne?
Lady Anne:	She is dying.
The Children:	How is Lady Anne?
Lady Anne:	She is dead!

With these words the child impersonating Lady Anne stretches on the floor, and the children gather around to see if she is indeed dead. Lady Anne comes to life. She jumps up and runs after the children. The child she catches becomes Lady Anne during the next game.

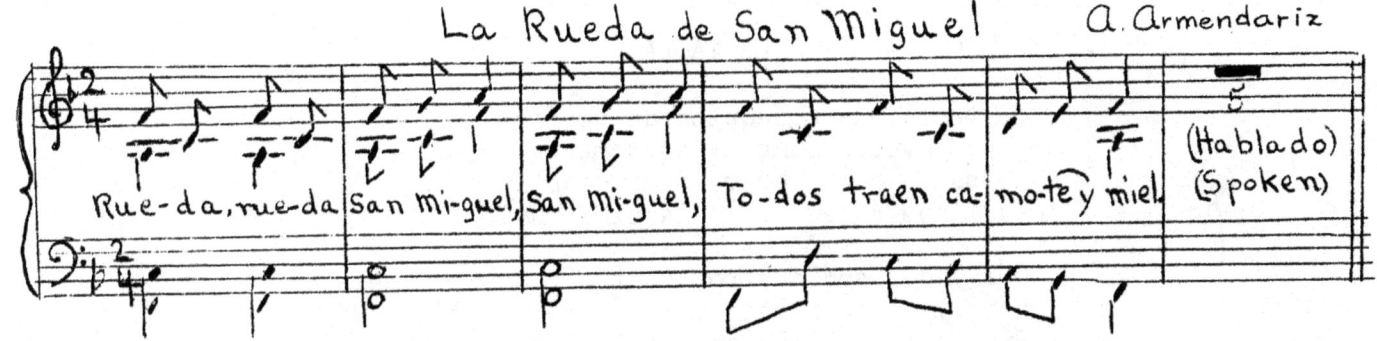

LA RUEDA DE SAN MIGUEL

Rueda, rueda de San Miguel, San Miguel
Todos traen camote y miel-
A lo maduro, a lo maduro
Que se voltee ———————— de burro.
         (nombre)

DIRECCIONES: No hay límite del número de niños que pueden jugar este juego divertido e interesante. Uno de los niños se coloca en el centro de un círculo formado por los demás. Éstos, cogidos de la mano le rodean al mismo tiempo cantando las primeras tres líneas de la canción. Cantándose las palabras "a lo maduro, a lo maduro" el niño que está en el medio canta la última línea y así indica uno de los de la rueda por nombre. Este niño debe voltearse cara para afuera y así seguir dando vueltas con los demás.

La canción se repite de este modo hasta que todos los niños están volteados cara para afuera. Ellos siguen dando vueltas acelerando el paso hasta que el círculo se corta por su misma velocidad y así se acaba el juego.

SAINT MICHAEL'S WHEEL

Round and round with San Miguel,
Bringing honey sweet to sell;
Get to your place...Get to your place...
———————— the donkey, turn your face.
    (name)

DIRECTIONS: Any number of children may play this game. One child stands in the center of a ring formed by the other children who, joining hands, walk round and round singing the first two lines of the song. After the words, "everyone ready," the child in the center of the circle sings the last line. The one named must immediately turn about, facing outward, and with hands still joined, continue to circle with the others.

The song is repeated until all the children face outward. They continue to circle, increasing the pace, until the ring is broken, ending the game in a gale of merriment.

LA TABLA

Yo tenía una muñequita de vestido azul
Con su velo blanco y su sombrero estul,
La saque a pasear y se me constipo
La lleve a la casa y la niña murió.

Dos y dos son cuatro, cuatro y dos son seis
Seis y dos son ocho y ocho diez y seis,
Brinca la tablita que ya la brinqué
Bríncala muchacha que yo ya pasé.

DIRECCIONES: Un gran número de niños pueden jugar este juego. El Guía se coloca adelante de los demás niños hechos línea. Los niños cantan el primer verso de la canción. El Guía comienza cantando el segundo verso: "Dos y dos son..." y apuntando a uno de los niños, el niño responde: "Cuatro."

El Guía:	Cuatro y dos son?...
El Niño:	Seis.
El Guía:	Seis y dos son?...
El Niño:	Ocho.
El Guía: (cantando)	Brinca la tablita que ya la brinqué
	Bríncala muchacha que yo ya pasé
	Ocho y ocho son?...
El Niño:	Diez y seis.

Si cualquier falta en dar la respuesta correcta, él o ella tiene de salirse a la línea y colocarse detrás del Guía. Las cuentas propuestas por el Guía en el último verso siguen hasta que haya faltado el último niño en dar la respuesta correcta. El niño que permanece hasta el fin será el Guía y sigue el juego adelante.

THE TABLE

Once I had a little doll all dressed in blue,
With a veil as white as snow and hat all new;
We went out a-walking and she moaned and cried,
I took her right home, but the poor baby died.

Two and two are four and four and two make six,
Six and two make eight and eight more you can mix;
Say your little table from the first to last,
Learn them well, muchacha, for you know I've passed.

DIRECTIONS: Several children play this game. The leader stands in front of the children who form a line. The children sing the first verse of the song and the leader begins the second verse: "Two and two are..." and pointing to a child, the child answers, "Four."

The Leader:	Four and two are?...
A Child:	Six.
The Leader:	Six and two are?...
A Child:	Eight.
The Leader sings:	This you mustn't mix.
	Learn to say your tables;
	I have learned mine.
	Eight and eight are?...
A Child:	Sixteen.

If a child fails to give the correct answer, he or she must leave the line and take a place behind the leader. The numbers of the last verse may be changed indefinitely. The last child in the line becomes the leader in the next game.

La Tabla

arr. by A. Armendariz.

VÍBORA DE LA MAR

Víbora, víbora, de la mar
Por aquí pueden pasar
Por aquí yo pasé
Y una niña dejaré.
Una niña cual será
La de adelante o la de atrás
La de adelante corre mucho
Y la de atrás se quedará.

DIRECCIONES: Los dos niños más altos del grupo se toman de las manos y las levantan en forma de arco. Los demás niños se forman en línea y pasan cantando por debajo del arco. Al cantarse las últimas palabras de la canción los dos, que forman el arco, bajan las manos así prendiendo al niño que vaya pasando debajo del arco. El niño, que ha sido prendido, tiene que adivinar cual de dos cosas ha sido escogida de antemano por los dos niños formando el arco. Si acaso él adivina, puede volver a la línea y el juego sigue adelante, pero si no, él o ella será multado y tiene de brincar en un pie inclinando la cabeza a cada uno de los demás niños o otra multa semejante.

SERPENT OF THE SEA

Sea serpent, sea serpent from the sea
You must follow, follow me;
Under this archway we now must glide,
And we'll leave a girl inside.
One little girl,---Oh, who can she be?
One ahead or back of me?
That one ahead,---how she runs away,
So that last one has to stay.

DIRECTIONS: The two tallest children in the group join hands and raise them to make an arch. The other children form in line and pass under the arch, singing as they go. At the last words of the song the two children who form the arch capture the child who happens to be passing under it. The child who is caught is asked to choose between two articles which the two children who formed the arch have agreed upon. If the proper answer is given, the child returns to the line and the game continues. If the child's guess is wrong he or she is penalized by hopping on one foot, nodding to each child in the line or a like action.

Víbora de la Mar
arr. by A. Armendaris.

Ví-bo-ra, ví-bo-ra de la mar, por a-qui pue-den pa-sar;
por a-qui yo pa-sé y un-a ni-ña de-ja-ré.

EL FLORÓN

El florón anda en las manos, en las manos,
Y en las manos lo han de hallar,
Adivinen quien lo tiene, quien lo tiene
O se queda plantón.

DIRECCIONES: En este juego todos menos dos de los niños están sentados en línea con sus manos detrás de ellos. Uno de los dos que no están sentados esconde una flor o un botón en la mano de uno de los niños mientras ellos cantan la canción "El Floron."

Cuando cesan de cantar, el otro niño parado adelante de la linea trata de adivinar cual de las manos extendidas encierra la flor o el botón. Si él adivina correctamente él luego cambia lugares con el niño que tenía la flor escondida. Pero si no adivina tiene que seguir adivinando hasta atinar.

THE FLOWER

In our hands a flower is hiding,
And it can be found some way;
You must guess the one who has it
Or you'll be the goose all day......

DIRECTIONS: Any number of children can play this guessing game. One is chosen "it," and one is chosen to place the flower in the children's hands. All but these two sit in a row with their hands behind them. The child who is "it" sits opposite the row, and, as the children in the row sing, the other child puts the "flower," or the small object to be hidden, into one of the open hands. When the singing stops, the child who is "it" begins to guess. If he is successful, he exchanges places with the child in whose hand the "flower" is found. If he does not guess correctly, the game continues as before.

El Florón

HILITOS DE ORO

DIRECCIONES: Este es un juego para las muchachas, pero un muchacho puede tomar la parte del Mensajero del Rey. Hay dos personajes principales, El Mensajero del Rey, y la Madre. Las Hijas, o las demás muchachas, se paran hechas fila detrás de la Madre. El Mensajero del Rey llega brincando en un pie y cantando así:

> Hilitos, hilitos de oro,
> Que se me vienen quebrando,
> Qué dice el Rey y la Reina
> Qué tantas hijas tendrá?

La Madre responde:

> Que tenga las que tuviere
> Que nada le importa al Rey.

El Mensajero se retira brincando en un pie y cantando:

> Yo ya me voy muy descontento
> A darle cuenta al Rey.

La Madre:

> Vuelva, vuelva caballero,
> No sea tan majadero
> Que de las hijas que yo tengo
> Escoja la más mujer.

El Mensajero:

> No escojo por bonita
> Ni tampoco por mujer
> Yo escojo una florecita
> Acabada de nacer.

Luego el Mensajero se acerca a la primera muchacha y dice: "Esta huele a rosa de castilla" y sigue con todas dándoles nombres de diferentes perfumes. Llegando a la última dice, "Esta huele a violeta, y ésta me llevo." Se la lleva y vuelve otra vez y se repite la misma acción como al principio, pero siempre el pide y les pone a las hijas los nombres de otras cosas como son frutas, o así como en la primera visita había pedido una florecita. Al fin llega a la última hija, la hija favorita, y dice:

> Y a ti escojo hija amada
> Que le seas a La Reina, criada.
> Ven y yo te llevaré
> Y bien te prometeré.

La hija favorita se para contra una pared con un leño trampado debajo de un pie. La Madre se le acerca y le pregunta: "Tienes arroz?" La Hija responde, "No." La Madre sigue preguntando: "Tienes ajo? Tienes pan? Tienes papas? Tienes frijoles?" etc. A todas las preguntas La Hija responde, "No." Hasta que La Madre le pregunta: "Tienes carne?" Donde La Hija responde "Sí." Y La Madre arrebata el leño y sale a huir con el. Las muchachas salen tras de ella gritando, en voz alta, y se acaba el juego.

LITTLE THREADS OF GOLD

DIRECTIONS: This game is usually played by girls, although the role of the King's Messenger (sometimes played by a group called the servants) may be played by a boy. Two leaders are chosen, the King's Messenger and the Little Mother, called Nana (term of endearment), whose daughters, the other children, form a row behind her. The King's Messenger, hopping on one foot and singing, approaches the group.

> A gossamer thread so golden,
> Oh, what shall we do to break it!
> The King and the Queen will take it
> When choosing your daughters fair.

When he comes to the row of girls, Nana sings:

> The Queen may have all she wishes,
> The King says it does not matter....

And the King's Messenger breaks in:

> But I wish that I might flatter
> His Majesty with this tale.

Then he hops away, and Nana sings:

> Good sir, please return, oh, please, sir,
> And do not appear so whining,
> From all of my daughters pining,
> You may choose the fairest one.

The King's Messenger returns, singing:

> Oh, I will not choose for manners
> Nor choose one who does her duty,
> For I would prefer a beauty,
> The one who is young and small.

He goes to the last girl in the row and pretending to smell her hair, says, "This one smells of wild rose," or "This one of violets," and so on down the line, giving each child the name of a fragrant flower. He returns to the girl at the end of the line and says, "This one I choose," placing her behind him. He again approaches the Little Mother and the same routine is followed, but each time he chooses a "daughter" he asks for something different, a bird or an animal, giving its color or quality. He finally chooses the last or favorite daughter and sings:

>O you will become the Queen's maid
>For that is the way the plan's laid
>Come now, and I'll show the right way
>A welcome you'll have today.

When all the daughters have been taken by the King's Messenger, the favorite daughter stands near a wall with a stick of wood under one partly extended foot. The Little Mother approaches her and asks, "Have you any rice?" "Beans?" "Have you any bread?" To each question, the favorite daughter answers, "No." But if the Little Mother asks, "Have you meat?" the favorite daughter answers, "Yes," whereupon the Little Mother snatches the stick of wood and darts away followed by the others screaming at top voice. And thus the game ends.

Hilitos, Hilitos de Oro

arr. by J. Armendariz

LA VIUDITA DE SANTA ISABEL

Está es la viudita
De Santa Isabel
Que quiere casarse
Y no sabe con quién.

El hijo del cura
Le mandó un papel
Y ella le mandó otro
De Santa Isabel.

Corriendo corriendo
Me di un tropezón
Por darle la mano
Le di el corazón.

Me gusta la leche
Me gusta el café
Pero más me gustan
Los ojos de usted.

DIRECCIONES: Un número de niños puede jugar este juego. A una niña se le da el nombre, La Viudita y a un niño se le da el nombre de, El Hijo del Cura. Estos dos se paran enfrente, el uno del otro, mientras los demás niños, hechos linea, cantan los primeros tres versos de la canción. Entonces el Hijo del Cura se adelanta un paso y canta los últimos dos versos. Los demás niños se hacen los que están corriendo, casi cayéndose, y al mismo tiempo ofreciéndole a La Viudita sus corazones. Ellos pretenden beber leche y luego café. Mientras se cantan las últimas dos lineas del último verso ellos se toman de la mano y bailan al rededor de La Viudita y el Hijo del Cura.

THE WIDOW OF SAINT ISABEL

This is the poor widow
Of Saint Isabel,
She wishes to marry
With whom she can't tell

The Parson's Son wrote her,
It pleased her quite well,
She sent him a letter
From Saint Isabel.

Oh I ran so swiftly
I 'most fell apart,
I held out my hand,
But I gave her my heart.

Oh, I like my coffee
And I like my tea,
But you know I give all
My true love to thee.

DIRECTIONS: A number of children play this game. A girl is chosen for the part of the Little Widow and a boy is chosen for that of the Parson's Son. These children stand opposite each other, while the other children form a line and sing the first three verses of the song. The Parson's Son steps forward and sings the last two verses. The children in the line carry out the motions of running, nearly falling, and giving their hearts to the Little Widow. They pretend to drink coffee and then tea. With the last lines of the last verse they join hands and dance around the Little Widow and the Parson's Son.

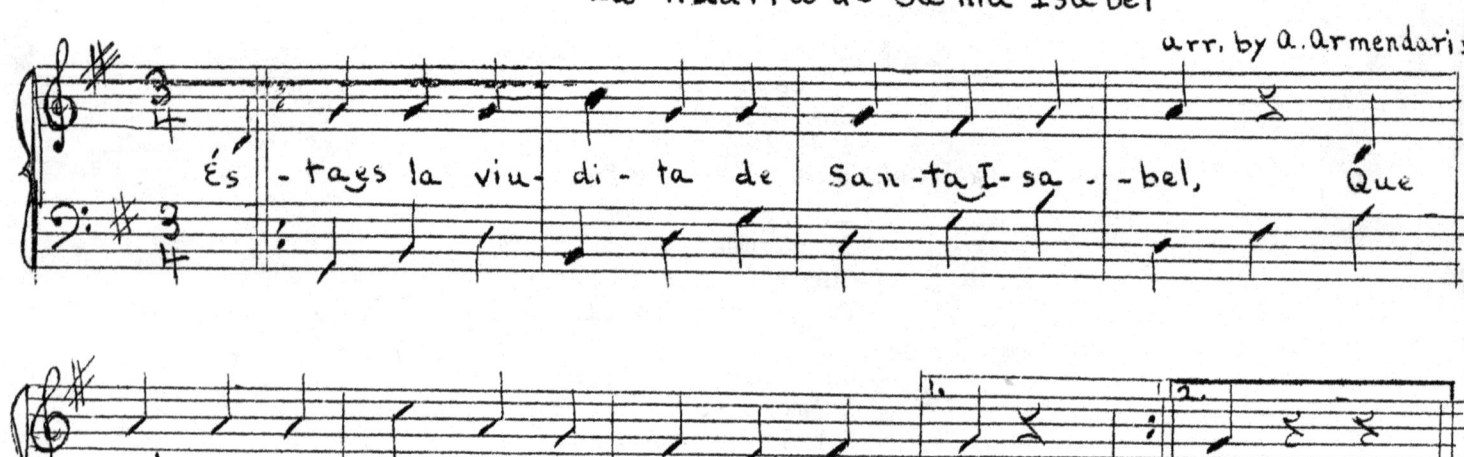

LA HUERFANITA

Pobrecita huerfanita
Sin su padre y sin su madre,
La echaremos a la calle
A llorar, su desventura.

Cuando yo tenía mis padres
Me paseaban en un coche,
Pero ahora que no los tengo
Me pasean en guangoche.

Cuando yo tenía mis padres
Me daban chocolate,
Y ahora que no los tengo
Me dan agua de metate.

Cuando yo tenía mis padres
Me vestían de oro y plata,
Y ahora que no los tengo
Me visten de hoja de lata.

DIRECCIONES: No hay límite del número de niños que pueden participar en este juego. La Huerfanita se escoge y se coloca en el centro de un círculo formado por los demás niños. A cada niño se le da el nombre de alguna materia, metal (siempre que sea de menos valor que la plata), palo, lana, algodón, y en fin. Los niños del círculo cantan el primer verso y al cantarse la tercer línea, La Huerfanita se arroja fuera del círculo. La Huerfanita canta los siguientes tres versos mientras ella da vuelta al trote fuera del círculo.

Al cantar La Huerfanita la tercer línea del último verso el niño designado por el nombre que se le ha dado, hoja de lata, plomo, cedro etc., trata de entrar al centro del círculo primero que La Huerfanita. Si logra hacerlo primero que La Huerfanita él toma el lugar de La Huerfanita y el juego sigue adelante.

LITTLE ORPHAN

Poor and homeless little orphan
With no father and no mother;
On the street we all will leave her,
She can cry like any other.

When my parents both were living,
In a coach we went out riding;
But now I have none to love me,
On a gunny-sack I'm riding.

When my parents both were living,
I had chocolate and candy;
But now I have none to love me,
I must take whatever's handy.

When my parents both were living,
I was clothed in gold and spangles,
Now I have no one to love me...
I wear scraps and cast-off bangles.

DIRECTIONS: Several children play this game. The Little Orphan is chosen and takes his or her place in the center of a circle formed by the other children. Each child bears the name of a substance, such as a metal (less in value than silver), wood, wool, cotton, etc. The children forming the circle sing the first verse. As they sing the third line, the Orphan breaks through the circle. The Orphan sings the second, third, and fourth verses as he or she trots around the circle. When the Orphan sings the third line of the last verse the child designated as "tin" (or whatever is named) must enter the circle before the Orphan. If the child is successful he or she will be the Orphan in the next game.

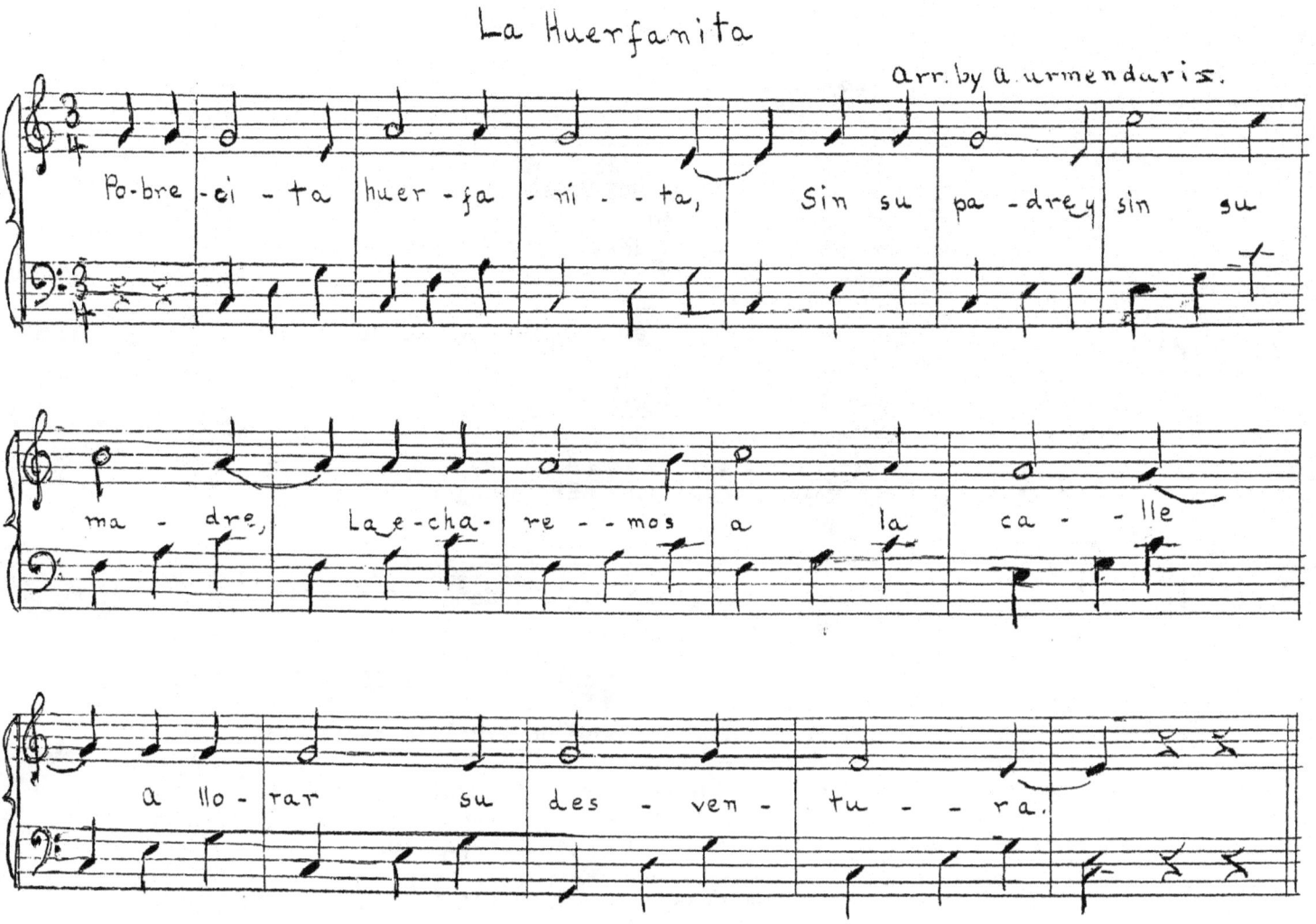

AMBO GATO

Ambo Gato, matarili rili ron
Qué quiere usted matarili rili ron
Quiero un paje matarili rili ron
Qué paje quiere matarili rili ron?
Quiero (nombre de niña) matarili rili ron
Qué nombre le pondremos, matarili rili ron
Le pondremos Rosa de Laurel, matarili rili ron
Aquí está mi hija
Con dolor de corazón
Celebremos, celebremos, todos juntos en la unión.

DIRECCIONES: En este juego dos guías se escogen; uno es el Ambo Gato (sus hijas son los pajes), y el otro es El Mensajero de la Corte Real. Los demás niños, los hijos de Ambo Gato, se toman de la mano y se paran en línea, detrás de la madre. El Mensajero se acerca y el diálogo que sigue se canta:

El Mensajero: Ambo Gato, matarili rili ron
Ambo Gato: Qué quiere usted, matarili rili?
El Mensajero: Quiero un paje matarili rili ron

Ambo Gato: Qué paje quiere matarili rili ron?

El Mensajero: Quiero (nombre de niña), matarili rili ron
Ambo Gato: Qué nombre le pondremos, matarili rili ron?
El Mensajero: Le pondremos (nombre de flor), matarili rili ron.
Ambo Gato: Aquí está mi hija, con dolor de corazón.

El niño o niña escogida sale de la línea y se pone junto al mensajero. Luego tomándose de las manos forman un círculo y bailan mientras cantan:

Celebremos, celebremos,
Todos juntos en la unión.

Cuando la última hija ha sido entregada al Mensajero se acaba el juego.

AMBO GATO

Ambo Gato, matarili rili ron
What do you wish sir? matarili rili ron (?)
I want a page, please, matarili rili ron
Which do you wish, sir? matarili rili ron
I want _____ (name), matarili rili ron
What shall we name her? matarili rili ron
Let's name her ___ (name), matarili rili ron
Here is my daughter, I hate to give her,
Let us make merry, matarili rili ron
Now all together, matarili rili ron.

DIRECTIONS: In this game two leaders are chosen; one is Ambo Gato, whose daughters are the pages, and the other is the Messenger from the Court. The children designated as Ambo Gato's daughters join hands and stand in a row behind their mother. The messenger approaches and the following dialogue is sung:

The Messenger: Ambo Gato, matarili rili ron
Ambo Gato: What do you wish sir? matarili rili
The Messenger: I want a page, please, matarili rili ron
Ambo Gato: Which do you wish, sir? matarili rili ron
The Messenger: I want _____ (name), matarili rili ron
Ambo Gato: What shall we name her? matarili rili ron
The Messenger: Let's name her ___ (name) matarili rili ron
Ambo Gato: Here is my daughter, I hate to give her.

The child chosen crosses from behind the mother to the messenger. All join hands and dance around in a circle as they sing:

Let us make merry, matarili rili ron
Now all together, matarili rili ron.

When the last daughter has been given to the messenger, the game ends.

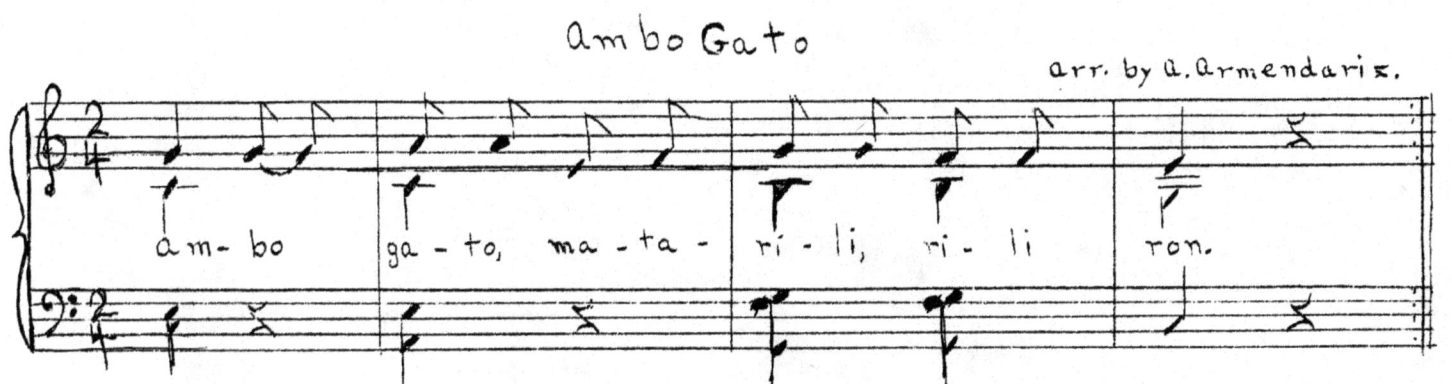

Ambo Gato

arr. by A. Armendariz.

***Spanish American Dance Tunes of New Mexico*, 1941, Unit No. 4**

Helen Chandler Ryan

```
SPANISH   AMERICAN

DANCE   TUNES

OF

NEW   MEXICO


WORK   PROJECTS   ADMINISTRATION

WPA  MUSIC  PROJECT

UNIT  NO. 4

1941
```

TABLE OF CONTENTS

Amor Ardiente . . . . . . Ardent Love (Waltz)
Camila (Camelia) . . . . Camelia
La Chinche . . . . The Bug
El Chotis . . . . The Schottisch
Cuadrilla . . . . Quadrille
    Parte I. . . . . Part I
    Parte II. . . . . . . Part II
    Parte III. . . . . . . Part III
    Parte IV. . . . . . . Part IV
    Parte V. . . . . Part V
    Parte VI. . . . . . . *Part VI
    Parte VII. . . . . . . Part VII

Cuna . . . . Cradle
Guadalupita . . . . Little Guadalupe
Indita . . . . Indian Maid
Jilote . . . . "Jilote"
Marcha Santa Ana . . . . Santa Ana March
El Paso Doble . . . . . . The Two Step
Polka No. 1 . . . . Polka No. I
Polka No. 2 . . . . Polka No. II
Polka No. 3 . . . . Polka No. III
La Raspa . . . . The New Mexico Shuffle
Rechumbe . . . . "Rechumbe"
Sombrero Blanco . . . . . White Hat
Talean . . . . "Talean"
Vals de Cadena (Chimayo) . Chain Waltz from Chimayo
Vals de los Panos No. 1 . Vals de los Panos No. I
Vals de los Panos No. 2 . Vals de los Panos No. II
Vals Español . . . . . . Spanish Waltz
Vaquero . . . . Cowboy
La Varsoviana . . . . . . The Varsoviana

                          * Part VI. repeat Part II.

Amor Ardiente. Vals

La Camila

La Chinche
(Rye Waltz)

Cuadrillas. Nº 1.

Cuadrillas. Nº 2.

Cuadrillas. Nº 3.

Cuadrillas Nº 4.

Cuadrillas. Nº 5.

Cuadrillas. Nº 6.

Cuadrillas. Cutilio or Nº 7.

La Cuna.

Guadalupita.

Indita

P. Valles arr.

El Jilote.

Marcha Santa Ana.

El Paso Doble.

Polka

P. Valles arr.

Polka.

Polka.

La Raspa

El Rechumbé.

Sombrero Blanco.

El Talean.

Vals de Cadena. (Chimayo)

El Vals de los Paños.

188

Vals de los Paños

El Vaquero

La Varsoviana.

Guitar Arrangements of Spanish American Folk Songs, 1939

GUITAR ARRANGEMENTS

of

SPANISH AMERICAN FOLK SONGS

Collected by the Federal Music Project of the
Works Progress Administration

The guitar method offered in this book has been worked out by Miss Eudora Garrett whose research and study was begun in Mexico with Francisco Salinas of the National Conservatory. Principles of guitar technique here set forth are based primarily on the teachings of Tarrega, acknowledged as the greatest Spanish guitarrist of all time, and on the later expositions of his pupil, Emilio Pujol.

This method is reccommended by the Federal Music Project of New Mexico for study and use throughout the state. It is hoped that this more standardized and complete system of instruction will aid in reviving the art of guitar playing as one worthy of its ancient Spanish tradition.

                                              Helen Chandler Ryan
                                              State Director
                                              Federal Music Project

                                              MARCH 1939

Manuel de Falla, speaking of the guitar:

> "Instrumento admirable, tan sobrio como rico, que aspera o dulcemente se aduena del espiritu, y en el que andando el tiempo se concentran los valores esenciales de nobles instrumentos caducados cuya herencia recoge sin perdida de su propio caracter de aquel que debe al pueblo por su origen."

This Spanish guitar, which the great Spanish composer praises so unreservedly, is an instrument that is particularly and uniquely New Mexico's own. Here the "tradition of Spain" is a living force, one that is manifested most clearly, perhaps, through its pure folk music--sung to the accompaniment of a guitar. The Federal Music Project in New Mexico emphasizes the importance of this instrument, not only for its ancient origin, its double aspect of popular and artistic utility and its vital influence on the evolution of instrumental music--but also because it typifies the artistic consciousness of the state; it is the Voice of New Mexico, in music.

One aim of the Project is the revival of a true Spanish guitar technique, since, in recent years, outside influences have caused foreign manners to predominate in popular playing. Also it is hoped to bring back into use, as far as is feasible, the true type of instrument to replace our present mixture of Hawaiian, American-factory and other hybrid shapes.

The true Spanish guitar is always played with the fingers, never with a pick; instead of wire strings, it should be strung with three gut strings in the treble and metal-wound silk ones in the bass. In place of our present cowboy guitar and banjo style of playing, its true technique is of two kinds, the "punteado" or picking style, in which the guitarrist uses his fingers to achieve the effects now attempted with a pick, and the almost forgotten "rasgueado" method which utilizes all fingers across all strings at one time, with additional percussion effects obtained by striking the wood of the guitar with the hands. In shape, the authentic instrument maintains a beautiful proportion, with a wider fingerboard than other types, and the lower bridge is made stationary on the sound box, with the strings attached at that point.

With many popular and inexpensive "Guitar Methods" now on the market, the task of coordinating instruction systems is a difficult one. Most of these books suggest either an incorrect position, or ignore this important matter entirely; few of them designate full chords, giving only those notes to be used in a certain style of playing, and no strokes are offered except those obtainable with a pick. Because of this lack of dependable methods, a simple, correct system of presenting guitar instruction is in the following pages, which all music project teachers are urged to follow. Except for certain basic fundamentals, most of the suggestions here offered have never been published.

NOTES ON THE USE OF THIS BOOK

The correct way to learn to play guitar is by note-reading, not merely by learning to follow diagrams of the proper chords. Therefore in these arrangements, in addition to naming the chord above the measure in which it is to be used, the treble notation of all chords is written throughout, with the hope that students will familiarize themselves with guitar music notation. All arrangements have been made in the simplest possible form, for clarity and practicability, and can be followed easily. Instructors can transpose the bass of other songs into the treble clef for additional studies.

On succeeding page will be found a diagram of the first position of the keyboard, offering a new plan of note placements worked out in the New Mexico Federal Music Project. Teachers will notice that the music staff has been inserted in each of the first five frets of the guitar keyboard, simplifying the process of locating various notes. It is suggested that large charts be made from this diagram and kept before guitar classes, since the visual association of note, name of note, and fret placement offer one of the easiest and most effective ways of mastering the difficult keyboard.

Transitions (short runs or notes in harmony) from one chord to another will be found in many of the songs. These add much to the beauty and variety of guitar accompaniments in the "punteado" style of playing. Students will be able to work out these "decorations" very quickly by means of the keyboard chart.

Limitations of the manuscript prevent any attempt at offering chord harmonies for solo guitar playing, so these arrangements serve only as guides to effective accompaniments for the simple melody line designated as "solo". The chart of simple guitar chords, giving the full tonic, 7th, and minor chords built on each note, are all that are needed for these arrangements.

The variety and interest of guitar accompaniments depend on the utilization of different strokes. Twenty separate stroke patterns are offered in this book, all of which can be worked out correctly if they are counted and executed in exact time, the way they have been analyzed. The student should master the basic "pick" strokes first, then the pure Spanish "rasgueado" style strokes and the combinations of both. These strokes, so far as is known, have never been published up to this time, and it is hoped that New Mexico guitar players will, with patience and practice, master them for a better style and a more interesting guitar technique.

GENERAL INSTRUCTION

Good guitar playing depends upon the observance of a few fundamental rules:
1. Learn the correct practice position, and keep it.
2. Make each note of every chord sound clear and full, allowing no "buzzes", indistinct tones, or uneven tempos.
3. Utilize as many strings as possible to achieve richness of tone.
4. Never become weary of working out new strokes, new effects.
5. Follow these rules and remember that the secret is -- "PRACTICE".

GUITAR POSITION

Holding the Guitar--Sit in a chair of proper height, one with no arms. Cross the right knee over the left, place the curve of the instrument on the curve of the thigh and hold the guitar closely against the body; lean over it slightly, if necessary at first, to see the keyboard. Never let the guitar slide from this position while practicing.

Right Arm--Support the right arm by placing the muscular part of the fore-arm (3 or 4 inches from the elbow) on the widest part of the guitar, slightly back of the line of the bridge. Let the muscle rest on the edge made by the front and side of the guitar (never on the front), to afford complete freedom for wrist and fingers. Do not let the guitar slip into the crook of the elbow.

Right Hand-- Leave wrist flexible for all "rasgueado" style playing either the thumb, one finger, or all fingers are being used across all strings. For "punteado" style playing, the thumb rests on the bass strings and the first three fingers on the treble strings. Keep the fingers and hand as nearly as possible at right angles to the strings.

Left Hand--Place the soft part of the thumb in the center of the underneath part of the fingerboard, so that the line of the thumb forms a "T" with the finger - board. Leave the thumb free for sliding up and down the fingerboard in this position. The left arm should be free and relaxed to afford easy movement of thumb and fingers. Bring the fingers over the strings with a circular movement of the hand, leaving as much space as possible between the palm of the hand and the strings...this exercise will demonstrate that even small children can reach all chords with ease if they work in the proper guitar position.

PRACTICE SUGGESTIONS

If a string buzzes or fails to sound distinctly, it is for one of three reasons: The finger is in the wrong place (it must be near the metal bar of the fret, not on it or up close to the upper bar), there is not sufficient pressure on the string, or some other finger is touching the string that does not sound.

Work on single note scales as well as chords, to stretch and strengthen the fingers in order to secure clear tones on each note.

GENERAL INSTRUCTION (Cont'd)

New Mexico guitar players, to maintain their tradition of fine Spanish guitar technique, should learn to play with the fingers and not with a pick. General rules for this method are as follows:

> For "punteado" style playing, always use the thumb on the three bass strings; after sounding a string, let the thumb rest on the next string (unless it is to be played in the treble).
> Avoid picking a string with an upward movement as this leaves the fingers in the air and position is lost for the next note.
> Use the first three fingers on the three treble strings, the 1st finger on the 3rd string, the 2nd on the 2nd string, and the 3rd finger on the 1st string. Learn first of all to pick these three strings in unison, getting a clear tone from each. The movement of the fingers should be upward, parallel with the guitar, and not outward, as this loses position for the next chord.
> For "rasgueado" style playing, master the "golpe" and "rasgueado" explained elsewhere.

In true Spanish guitar playing, the thumb of the left hand is never used to play bass notes except very rarely in the execution of classical guitar works. All students should be taught, from the first lesson, to make the bar or "ceja" with the first finger holding down all the strings in a given fret; by this means all strings can be used without discord and the thumb is not necessary. There are simpler ways of playing an F chord, a G Minor, &c., but it is preferable always to "conquer the ceja" for fuller chords and better technique. Practice first on the half-bars of the chords of D and A7th, and the full bar can be mastered quickly.

With certain chords, as indicated by an "x" on the chord diagrams, the 6th string is not used. In these cases (chords of D, D7th and D Minor) use the 4th and 5th bass strings. When playing C, C7th, B7th or the simplified F (not diagrammed but allowed for in the song arrangements in this key), move the bass finger from one string to another as indicated.

Advanced students are advised to secure a "capo" or bar for use in playing in the "flat keys". To play in the key of B flat (2 flats) place the capo on the 1st fret and play as in A; to play in E flat (3) place capo on 1st fret and play as in D; to play in A flat (4) place capo on 1st fret and play as in the key of G.

From the lists of chord progressions "used in this key" on the chord diagram, students should learn to substitute the corresponding chords in other keys and transpose songs into various keys for practice in chord progression. Chords are listed in order of each note of the scale for better ease in finding the various patterns.

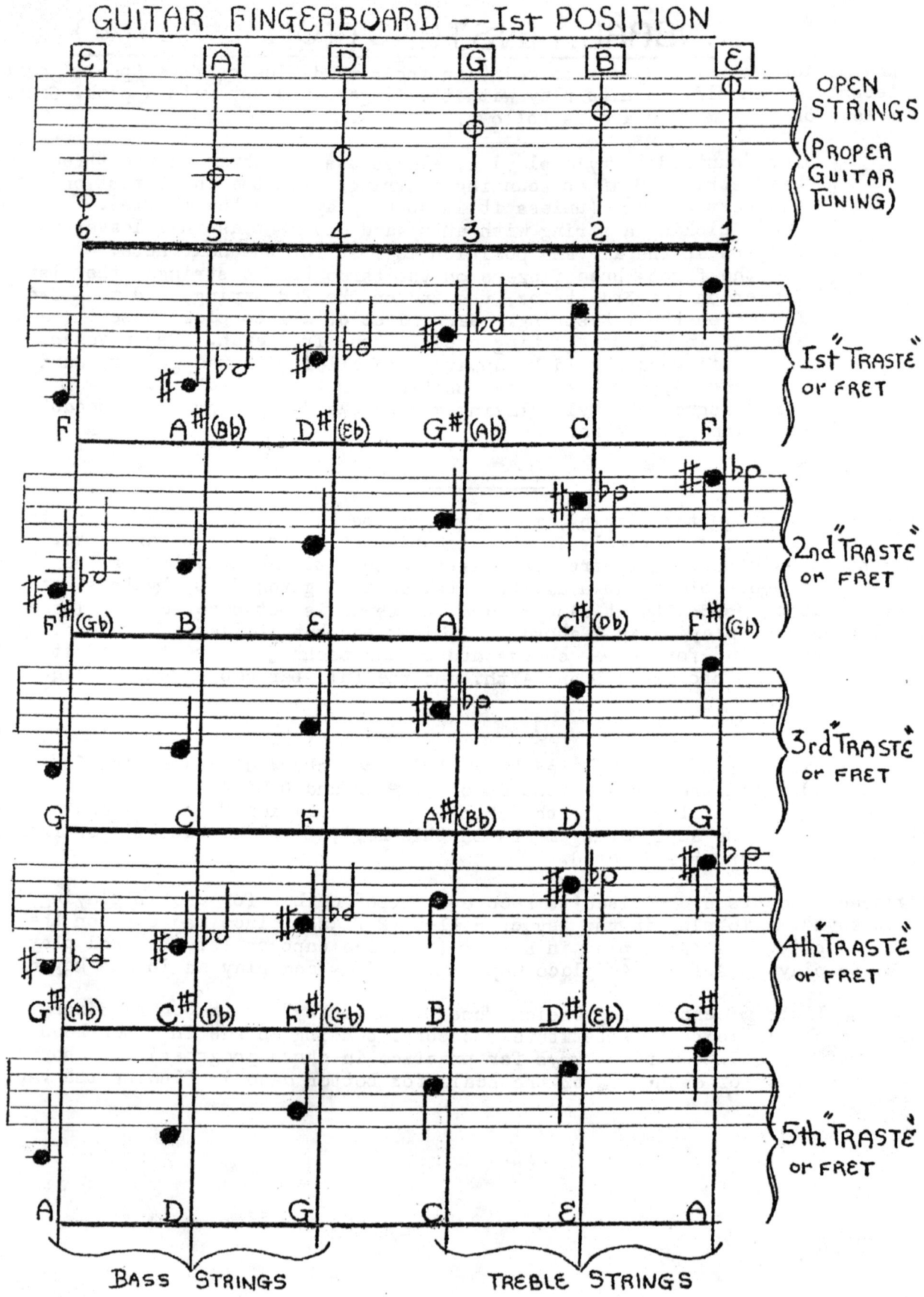

GUITAR CHORDS

TONIC CHORDS	CHORDS OF THE 7th	MINOR CHORDS	chords used in this key
C	C7	CM	C–G7–F
G–#	G7	GM	G–D7–C
D–##×	D7 ×	DM ×	D–A7–G
A 3#	A7	AM	A–E7–D
E 4#	E7	EM	E–B7–A
B 5#	B7	BM	B–F#7–E
F–♭	F7	FM	F–C7–B

GUITAR STROKES

STROKES IN 2-4 TIME	TANGO STROKES (2-4 & 4-4 Time)
A) Basic Stroke: 1- Pick 5th in bass (always with thumb). &- Pick treble strings. 2- Pick 6th in bass. &- Pick treble strings. B) Combination Stroke: 1- Pick 5th in bass. &- Down treble strings with 1st finger. a- Up treble strings with 1st finger. 2- Pick sixth in bass. &- Pick treble strings. C) Combination Stroke: 1- Pick 5th in bass. &- Slow Rasgueado. a- Complete Rasgueado of above beat. 2- Pick 6th in bass. &- Pick treble strings. D) Basic Stroke, Second Type: 1- Down, all strings, with thumb. &- Golpe, all strings, with fingers. 2- Down, all strings, with thumb. &- Golpe, all strings, with fingers. E) Development of Basic Stroke D: 1- Down all strings with thumb. &a- Slow Golpe. 2- Down all strings with thumb. &- Down all strings with fingers. (Accent Golpe for syncopation effect.) F) Rumba Type Stroke: 1- Down, all strings, with thumb. &- Up, all strings, with 1st finger. 2- Down all strings, all fingers. &- Down all strings, all fingers.	G) Simple Tango Stroke: 1- Down all strings, with thumb. &- Silence strings with hand. 2- Down all strings, with thumb. &- Silence strings with hand. H) Basic 4-4 Tango Stroke: 1- Pick 5th in bass. &2- Rest. &- Pick 4th in bass. 3- Pick treble strings. &- Rest. 4- Pick 6th in bass. &- Rest. I) Combination Tango Strokes: 1- Down, all strings, with thumb. &- Silence all strings with hand. 2- Rest. &3- Slowly up all strings, 1st finger. &- Rest. 4- Pick 6th in bass. &- Rest. J) Development of Stroke H: 1- Down, all strings, with thumb. 2- Rest. 3- Rasgueado. 4- Golpe, all strings, with fingers. K) Additional 4-4 Time Stroke, Jazz Type 1- Down, all strings, with thumb. 2- Golpe, all strings. &- Up, all strings, with 1st finger. a- Down, all strings, all fingers. 3- Down, all strings, with thumb. 4- Down, all strings, all fingers. (Accent beats 1&4 for special effect.)

GOLPE: A quick movement of all fingers across all strings of the guitar. It is best practiced and mastered by holding the hand closed (fist shape) about one inch above the strings, then opening the fingers one by one "as if flipping water". The little finger should cross the strings first, followed by the others so that the movement of each finger across each string is heard distinctly in a rolling, strumming effect.

RASGUEADO: Same movement as the Golpe, except the roll of each finger is even more pronounced and drawn out. In popular terms a "rasgueado" is a down movement of all fingers followed by a very quick up movement across all strings with the thumb. The two motions usually are compassed in one time beat, not two separate counts. Guitar notation for the 3 types of "rasgueados" (descending - with all fingers; ascending - with the thumb, or this last mentioned combination of both) is: in the urged to these ↑ ↕ ↑ ↓ or ↝ Only a few such notations will be found songs in this book, but the student is master this style of playing and use strokes wherever fitting.

GUITAR STROKES (Cont'd)

STROKES IN 3-4 TIME	HUAPANGO STROKES (6-8 TIME)
L) Basic Stroke: 1- Pick 5th in bass. 2- Pick treble strings. 3- Pick treble strings. (Repeat, using 6th in bass, then 5th, &c.) M) Combination Stroke: 1- Pick 5th in bass. &- Rest. 2- Down, all strings, with 1st finger. &- Up, all strings, with 1st finger. 3- Down, all strings, with 1st finger. &- Up, all strings, with 1st finger. (In alternate measures use Stroke L, substituting 6th in bass for 5th.) N) Combination Stroke: 1- Pick 5th in bass. 2- Golpe, all strings. 3- Up, all strings, with thumb. (In alternate measures use Stroke L, substituting 6th in bass for 5th.) O) Development of Basic Stroke: 1- Pick 5th in bass. &- Rest. 2- Pick 1st two treble strings. &- Pick 3rd string with first finger. 3- Pick 6th in bass. &- Pick 1st two treble strings. P) Slow Waltz Stroke: 1- Down all strings, with thumb. &- Rest. 2- Up, all strings, with 1st finger. &- Down, all strings, with 1st finger. 3- Down, all strings, with thumb. &- Up, all strings, with 1st finger.	(These strokes are popular for songs that are adaptable to their fast rhythm. With an unlimited variety of patterns possible -students can be encouraged to "invent" others than are given here.) Q) Simple Huapango Stroke: 1- Slap wood of guitar, just below strings, with fingers and palm. 2- Pull 1st finger up across all strings. 3- Down across all strings, 1st finger. (4, 5 & 6, --repeat above. Work to keep stroke even at a very fast tempo.) R) Variation on Stroke Q: 1- Thumb down across all strings. 2&3- 1st finger up and down in circular motion to achieve proper speed. S) Combination Stroke: 1- Slap wood of guitar as in Stroke Q. 2- Up, all strings, with 1st finger. 3- Down, all strings, with 1st finger. 4- Down, all strings, with thumb. 5- Up, all strings, with 1st finger. 6- Down, all strings, with 1st finger. (This stroke is effective with finger movements made up and down the keyboard.) T) Characteristic Huapango Stroke: 1- Golpe. 2- Up, all strings, with 1st finger. 3- Hit strings with hand closed. 4- Unfold fingers in golpe. 5- Rest. 6- Rest. (Vary with down thumb beat after Golpe, leaving only one count rest at end.)

EL BORRACHITO

EL BORRACHITO - 2 (Guitar)

EL DIA DE TU SANTO

EL DIA DE TU SANTO - 2 (Guitar)

LAS CAMPANAS DE BELEN

ME CASÉ CON UNA POCHA

CHAPARRITA

Note

The second page of the original of this guitar arrangement of *Chaparrita* was missing from the source material. In order to complete the song, the second page of this song from Unit 1 has been substituted.

LA LADERA

LA LADERA - 2 (Guitar)

CORRIDO DEL INDIO VICTORIO

SOÑANDO

EL AMOR DE LAS MUJERES

www.ingramcontent.com/pod-product-compliance
Lightning Source LLC
Chambersburg PA
CBHW080440170426
43195CB00017B/2833